WITHDRAWN

THE MEANING OF
THE WITCH OF ATLAS

THE MEANING OF
THE WITCH OF ATLAS

By CARL GRABO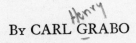

ASSOCIATE PROFESSOR OF ENGLISH

UNIVERSITY OF CHICAGO

CHAPEL HILL

THE UNIVERSITY OF NORTH CAROLINA PRESS

1935

To WRITE A BOOK, even though a small one, to elucidate a
light and fanciful poem of but seventy-eight stanzas demands
of its author some justification or apology. The most pedantic
mind might blush at so gross a redundancy. Or, if the poem
is difficult, its laborious interpretation should be at least simple and clear. An obscure book, though short, is a thankless
annotation upon an obscure poem. These criticisms I foresee
and can only reply, in mitigation of my offense, that I had
hoped at the outset to write a much simpler book than this,
but found that it was impossible for me to do so. Let me
explain why.

The obstacle to brevity and simplicity lies in the present
state of Shelleyan criticism. Shelley's language of symbol, his
background of neo-Platonism and science, and the character
of his creative imagination are all as yet little apprehended
even by specialists. It is they, first, who must be converted to
a new point of view, before they will concede, in their annota-
tions to Shelley, meanings which the general reader and lover
of poetry may accept. The general reader may dislike the
specialist and denounce him as one who destroys the poetic
character of poetry, but the specialist is nevertheless a necessity. He it is who does the grubbing underground and lays
the foundations for the aesthetic edifice of criticism. No doubt
he becomes often somewhat of a mole in the pursuit of his
business and his aesthetic judgments are not to be relied upon.
His business is not primarily to tell why a line of poetry is
beautiful but to show what it means—often a difficult matter
and one involving the history of human thought. There are,
to be sure, readers of poetry who seemingly wish not to know
what a poem means and who extract from it only some vague
emotional titillation. Critics of this order fell upon an earlier

Gnostic redivivo ? (handwritten marginalia)

book of mine and denounced me as one who labored to destroy the beauty of Shelley in my humble effort to make him intelligible. I derive comfort from remembering that Shelley was a neo-Platonist, one to whom intellectual clarity was synonymous with beauty. He would be little pleased with admirers who love him for his vagueness.

Why then, if Shelley so loved clarity, are some of his greater poems difficult? There are two forms of obscurity. One is born of simple muddle-headedness; the other is born of difficult and subtle ideas, or of an unfamiliar language. Shelley is difficult partly because he had a subtle mind which played with fine distinctions of thought, but more because he came gradually to the employment of a language with which most modern readers are wholly unfamiliar. He developed a symbolic form of expression which must be studied to be understood; its derivation must be traced. It was inconsiderate of Shelley in *Prometheus* and the *Witch of Atlas* to express himself recondidtely, but there was much justification for his doing so. The readers of his day treated him with indifference or contempt. For the most part they failed wholly to understand even his simpler poems. What reason had he, when he wished to please himself in his writing, to consider them?

We have, then, for the understanding of *Prometheus Unbound* and the *Witch of Atlas,* to learn Shelley's use of symbols and their neo-Platonic derivation. The meaning of the symbols can be conveyed in simple language and briefly, if the reader will take their interpretation on trust. This he cannot be expected to do until they are no longer questioned but are an accepted convention. The scholar and specialist must have passed upon them, certified them, and approved their translation. I have had, therefore, in interpreting the symbols of the *Witch* to cite evidence, sufficient evidence to convince the sceptical. Whether I have given too much evidence or too little, and whether I have argued the case too elaborately or too briefly, I cannot determine. I have endeavored to err on the side of brevity, to cite, from the vast mass of proofs available, sufficient but not too much; I have tried not to argue the case too tediously. Often I have laid the proofs before the reader and left it for him to discern their pertinency.

But with the acceptance of the symbols, and agreement as to the background of Shelley's thought, some of his work will nevertheless remain difficult for many readers. The Shelley of *Prometheus* and the *Witch* is an intellectual Shelley living in a world of his own making. He has his philosophy and theology built of materials derived from several sources and blent into a unity which may be called a system. This is set forth fully and profoundly in *Prometheus Unbound.* The *Witch of Atlas* is a playful fantasy upon themes announced in the profounder work. The two poems are mutually illuminating; interpretations of either are corroborative of the other.

Nevertheless the study of the *Witch* is the best preface to the study of *Prometheus,* for familiarity with Shelley's symbolism makes the language of *Prometheus* easier to grasp and permits the reader to concern himself with the ideas, which are philosophical and profound. The order of my own investigations has been otherwise. The study of Shelley's use of science in *Prometheus* was followed by an interpretation of the poem in its entirety and with the gathering of an extensive apparatus of appendices prepared for the convenience of the Shelley student. So considerable a volume has had, in these times, to remain in manuscript while I wrote the present small volume upon the *Witch.* I am not sorry, now, for the delay. My book upon Shelley's science, and the present work, corroborative of the earlier findings and introducing also Shelley's neo-Platonic symbolism, are the best prelude to the more difficult interpretation of *Prometheus*.

There are many lovers of Shelley the lyric poet who may not care for Shelley the philosopher. They will enjoy his ordinary speech and dislike his cryptic language of symbol. Some will even resent this other, this intellectual Shelley. They will feel that a poet should be simple if he wishes to be understood. It is a justifiable attitude. Yet the effort to understand the symbolic language and the philosophy which synthesizes neo-Platonism and science is very greatly rewarded. The inner world of Shelley's thought is strange and beautiful. His interpretation of the universe in the two poems *Prometheus* and the *Witch* is complete. We get from him, as from the greatest writers and philosophers, an attitude of mind, a way of regarding experience. We are released from our own mental universe into another, a vaster and more beautiful universe which is the creation of a beautiful and great mind.

I wish to express my thanks to Professor Alexander Cappon of Montana State College, and to Professor John D. Scheffer of Augustana College, Sioux Falls, South Dakota, for their assistance in preparing this manuscript for the press; also to Professor George L. Marsh and Mr. Martin J. Freeman of the University of Chicago for their assistance with the proofs.

CARL GRABO

University of Chicago.

TABLE OF CONTENTS

THE MEANING OF
THE WITCH OF ATLAS

CHAPTER I

THE NATURE OF THE *WITCH OF ATLAS*

> My Witch ...
> .....
> ...took ... three days
> In dressing.
> .....
> If you unveil my Witch, no priest nor primate
> Can shrive you of that sin,—if sin there be
> In love, when it becomes idolatry.
> —*W. of A.* ll. 33-48.

THREE DAYS only in the making, the *Witch of Atlas* is hewn from the same block from which were fashioned the gigantic *Prometheus* and the lesser *Cloud*. All three works are born of the same philosophy, employ the same symbols, and reflect equally the Shelley whose philosophy is mature, who has synthesized his radical social philosophy with his neo-Platonism, and has added thereto, to round out his picture of the universe, the speculations of science in meteorology and electricity. The *Witch of Atlas,* written in a gay mood and with that extraordinary facility which Shelley so often displays, is only superficially a light creation. Back of it lies all of Shelley's reading and all his thought. For its full interpretation is needed an interpretation of the *Cloud* and of *Prometheus* as it in turn illuminates these. Beneath its airy dress it is profoundly philosophical. To its understanding must be brought to bear knowledge of Egyptian and Greek myth and the rationalization thereof; knowledge of the neo-Platonists and their symbolism; knowledge of the discoveries and speculations of Shelley's day in electricity and meteorology.

Who or what is the Witch? What answer can we make to Shelley's gay challenge? Guesses at least we can hazard,

[3]

guesses which verge on probability or certainty, though to establish this probability with proofs to convince the sceptical promises to be a long and laborious process. The Witch, perhaps, is Asia in her youth before her union with Prometheus, the mind of man, in a regenerate world. The Witch is the spirit of love and beauty in nature. She is the earthly Venus, born of the sun and a sea nymph. She is aërial electricity born of water vapor sucked by the sun from the sea. She is Isis, the Moon goddess, presiding over rains and dews and the fertility of earth watered by the Nile. Her sphere is all beneath the Moon. She is Juno, goddess of the lower heavens, or Minerva the grey-eyed, goddess of the air and of wisdom, raising the souls of men from material things to the enduring life of the intellect symbolized by that ethereal earth which is the moon. She is the spirit of animation in nature, goddess of love, and marriage, and fertility; conserver of the seeming dead; inspirer of dreams, creating, by some magic power of the imagination, in the forms of material things semblance of the divine archetypes. She is the creative spirit of intellectual beauty.

I have thus put in the form of assertion some of the conclusions at which, in the course of this study, I shall arrive. They will not be therein so dogmatically put but rather will be established as possibilities or probabilities. It is not especially important that any one of them should be accepted as certain. The poem is fluid and shimmering, revealing many things under a changing sky. Yet the mind which created it was highly intellectual. Behind that mind is a body of myth and philosophy which can be examined; the symbols therein employed may be learned, and the derivation and use of these symbols by the poet be understood. Light thrown on the creative process will illumine the poem and make it as intelligible in measured statement as it is perhaps desirable any

work of art should be. In the instance of Shelley the defect
of criticism has been an over-stress of emotion, of fancy, of
irrational sportiveness. The essential intellectual basis for all
his imaginings has been too little understood. If, in this study,
the emphasis is throughout upon abstractions, upon ideas and
their poetic symbols, it will but serve somewhat to correct a
mistaken emphasis. Shelley too often is thought of even in
this day as passionate, emotional, fanciful, unintellectual, un-
disciplined. This study will, I trust, a little dispel these mis-
conceptions.

A casual reading of the *Witch of Atlas* reveals certain obvious things. It has to do in some way with Greek and
Egyptian mythology. The mother of the Witch is one of the
Atlantides. The Witch has relations with the Greek gods and
demi-gods of nature. But her activities bear also upon the
Nile and the Nile valley. An examination, then, of Greek and
Egyptian myth and the inter-relations of the two is a first
essential. The scientific and neo-Platonic elements are likewise, however, evident in the poem. It seems, therefore, that
to trace somewhat the rationalization of myth and to endeavor in its interpretation to follow both its physical and its
metaphysical readings, will illuminate the field of Shelley's
imaginings and discover the symbols which he employed and
their derivation.

The rationalization of myth is an ancient practice. If the
neo-Platonists are to be believed, Plato interprets the Greek
mythology metaphysically, and Homer even, in the *Odyssey,*
conveys profound philosophical truths. That the latter belief
is warranted may well be doubted, but its truth or falsity is of
no especial importance to our inquiry. It is enough that the
enlightened pagan world looked upon its myths as a modern
Christian may look upon the book of Genesis or the story of
Jonah: as fables not to be taken literally whatsoever their

spiritual implications. These myths the rationalists or the mystics variously interpreted in physical or metaphysical terms. A short survey of some typical interpretations will serve to supply the background before which we may subsequently work out a more detailed examination of the minutiae of the *Witch of Atlas*.

CHAPTER II

PHYSICAL AND METAPHYSICAL INTERPRETATION OF MYTH

DIODORUS SICULUS

Dᵢₒdₒᵣᵤₛ Siculus in his account of the ancient Egyptians, in part identifies their myths with Greek myths, in part ascribes to Egyptian deities a legendary pseudo-historical origin, and in part interprets the gods as symbols of natural forces. Fire, he says, is called by interpretation Vulcan; the earth wherein all things are made is Metera or Demeter. Water, called Oceanus, is to the Egyptians identical with the Nile, the nourishing mother of all. Vulcan, being the first to discover the use of fire, is said by some to be the first of the Egyptian kings.

After Vulcan, it is said, Saturn reigned, married his sister Rhea and begat Osiris and Isis, but others say Jupiter and Juno. These latter became parents of Osiris, Isis, Typhon, Apollo, and Venus. Osiris is interpreted as Bacchus and Isis as Ceres. Osiris married Isis and in his reign improved the lot of man. Isis made many laws for men, restraining them from violence, and therefore is called Ceres, the lawgiver, by the Greeks. Isis is also identified with the moon, as is Osiris with the sun, and is thus the moist or generative principle in nature acting in conjunction with the fire of the sun, for "moisture generates creatures from heat, as from a seminal principle, things so generated, by being inwrapt in the dewy mists of the night, grew and increased, and in the day solidated, and were made hard by the heat of the sun."[1]

Isis is known sometimes as Ceres, sometimes as Luna, and

[1] *The Historical Library of Diodorus the Sicilian* . . . (trans. by G. Booth), I, 16.

[7]

at others as Juno. She was expert in the discovery of med-
icines beneficial to man, and having become a goddess continues to aid him, manifesting herself in sleep and curing
those in need of her. It is said also that she has found a
medicine which will raise the dead and make them immortal.

"To the air they gave the name of Minerva . . . and called
her the daughter of Jupiter, and counted a virgin, because the
air naturally is not subject to corruption, and is in the highest
part of the universe."[2] Also "They report that this goddess
lived a virgin all her days and that being likewise endued
with extraordinary wisdom, she found out many arts and sciences." She is described as living on an island in "a pleasant
and very large grotto . . . arched over with an exceeding high
and craggy rock, bespangled with stones of divers resplendent
colours." Round about grow many wonders, trees always
green, the home of ravishing birds. In the grotto "in every
part enlightened by the bright rays of the sun," grow flowers
and plants, some "that perpetually preserve their sweet odours
in their natural strength." No flower or leaf is to be seen
withered or decayed.[3]

We read also in Diodorus of the Atlantides, of interest to
us inasmuch as the mother of the Witch of Atlas was one of
them. These are daughters of Atlas, by name Maia, Electra,
Taygeta, Asterope, Merope, Halcyone, and Celaeno. These
maidens make various celestial alliances and become the moth-
ers of gods and demi-gods. That the term was loosely used,
however, is apparent from this quotation: "Nymphs were
commonly called Atlantides, because nymphs is a general
term in this country applied to all women."[4]

Even greater interest attaches to the account of the goddess
Cybele, of disputed but seemingly celestial ancestry. Exposed

[2] *Ibid.*, p. 21.
[3] *Ibid.*, pp. 209-10.   [4] *Ibid.*, p. 202.

as an infant in the mountain Cybelus, she is nourished by the wild beasts and grows to maturity. "The young lady growing up both in strength and years, was admired by all for her beauty, modesty, and ingenuity: for she was the first that invented the pipe, composed of many reeds, and the timbrel and cymbal, in sports and dances: she taught likewise how to cure (by purging) diseases both in children and cattle.

"For her extraordinary love to children, whom she often restored to health, by singing and lulling them in her arms, she was called by all the *Mother of the Mount*."[5]

There is account also of an island "under the arctic pole, where the Hyperboreans inhabit."[6] Here the climate is temperate and the soil rich. Latona, it is said, was born in this favored spot. "They say, moreover, that the moon in this island seems as if it were near to the earth, and represents in the face of it excrescences like spots in the earth."[7]

This is all that need be cited from Diodorus Siculus save three details of possible interest. For one, Prometheus is said to be a legendary king of Egypt whose lands are destroyed by floods in the river Eagle. Hercules diverts the stream and thus frees Prometheus.[8] The hermaphrodite, which is also important to Shelley and the interpretation of Shelley's works, is likewise mentioned by the historian. "Hermaphroditus . . . being sprung from Hermes and Aphrodite, was, from their two names joined together, so called."[9] And last there is a description of a lake which is like the magic fountain wherein the Witch bathes secure from the wintry winds. "For they say there [Ethiopia] is a four-square lake, an hundred and sixty feet in circuit, the water of which is in color like unto vermilion, and of an extraordinary sweet flavour, much like

[5] *Ibid.*, p. 199.
[6] *Ibid.*, p. 139.
[7] *Ibid.*
[8] *Ibid.*, p. 25.
[9] *Ibid.*, p. 223.

unto old wine; yet of such wonderful operation, that whosoever drinks of it goes presently mad, and confesses all the
faults that ever he had been before guilty of; but some will
scarce believe this relation."[10]

For these excerpts I have chosen passages which may in
later discussion of the *Witch of Atlas* prove useful: as in the
identification of her parentage, her place of residence, her attributes and employments. The phenomena have to do with
the moon, the air, with the generative and curative powers of
deity. It suffices at this point to say no more. I do not wish
to anticipate the debate which must later be conducted upon
the crucial points of the poem. Yet neither is it needful to
keep the reader in any doubt as to the bearing of this historical
survey. In the rationalization of myth and in its metaphysical
interpretation, the physical phenomena surrounding the Witch
in Shelley's description of her home and her activities are the
obvious starting points of our investigation.

PLUTARCH

Plutarch in his theosophical essays rationalizes the Egyptian
myths both in physical and metaphysical terms. Osiris symbolizes both the Nile and the sun. In his decline, during the
winter months, the sun retires to the Southern hemisphere and
the Nile is mastered by the drought, symbolized by Typhon.
At this time Isis, which is the moon, and also the moist principle, cherishes Horus, phase of the returning and triumphant
sun, lest he be wholly destroyed by Typhon. Isis is thus the
mediator, reconciling the extremes of the fiery and moist principles essential to fertility.[11]

"For they are of opinion," says Plutarch, "that to the lights
of the Moon the risings of the Nile bear a certain analogy."[12]

[10] *Ibid.*, p. 111.
[11] *Plutarch's Morals: Theosophical Essays* (trans. by C. W. King), p. 34.
[12] *Ibid.*, p. 37.

Thus the greatest rising of twenty-eight cubits is the measure of the moon's monthly revolution. Apis is the animated image of Osiris, "and he is conceived when a generative light falls strongly from the Moon, and touches a cow that is in heat."[13] The power of Osiris is within the moon, and his entrance thereto symbolizes the beginning of spring. Isis, indeed, is hermaphroditic, being in a sense both the male and the female principle. She is impregnated by the sun, "and again she emits and disseminates in the air generative principles."[14]

Various rites and symbols designate the moon and the sun in their several phases throughout the year and the relation of these to the seasons, to the waters of the Nile, and to the productive cycle of the earth. Throughout, Osiris is the beneficent principle warred upon by Typhon, and the rôle of Isis is to cherish and protect, she in her waxings and wanings bearing an elaborate relationship to Osiris. Typhon, author not only of droughts but of whirlwinds, earthquakes, and pestilences, wars upon sun and moon, the monthly waning of the moon and her occasional eclipse symbolizing his momentary triumph until she is again restored by Osiris, the sun.

In Plutarch, as in subsequent interpreters of myth, Isis, the moist, the generative principle, is the deity of lovers. "The constitution and beauty of Earth attracts the moon, and she is of influence in matters and over persons upon Earth, by reason of her relationship and proximity."[15] The vehicles both of sun and moon are boats, "expressing allegorically their nourishment and origin from moisture."[16] For water in this cosmology is thought of as the origin of all things. Further symbolical interpretation Plutarch concedes thus: "These are such as pretend, like the Greeks, that Saturn symbolizes *Time,* Juno the *Air,* the birth of Vulcan, the change of Air into

---

[13] *Ibid.*
[14] *Ibid.*

[15] *Ibid.,* p. 210.
[16] *Ibid.,* pp. 28-29.

Fire; and similarly amongst the Egyptians, that Osiris is the
Nile, copulating with Isis the *Earth;* Typhon the *Sea,* into
which the Nile flowing vanishes and is dispersed. . . ."[17]

Thus sufficiently for the physical interpretation of myth.
The metaphysical has been all but explicit in the conflict of
Osiris and Typhon, the good and evil principles at eternal
war. Plutarch further advances his interpretation in metaphysical terms which anticipate the thought and symbols of
the neo-Platonists. Thus Isis is Earth, Typhon is Tartarus,
Osiris is love.[18] All that lies below the moon is a dualism, a
mixture of good and evil in perpetual conflict. "The Universe
(if not the whole, yet that which surrounds Earth, and lies
below the Moon), is made inconsistent with itself, and variable and susceptible of frequent changes."[19] In this conception
the lunar world is the battlefield of the actions of reason and
wisdom inspired by the moon, with violence and force deriving from the sun. Sun and moon, in this reading, are at
variance. "The Sun is set on fire, and derives his nutriment
from the sea, whereas to the Moon the fountain and lacustrine
waters send up a sweet and gentle exhalation."[20]

A different reading of the myth, though again metaphysical, identifies Osiris with the divine intellectual principle.
"He Himself dwells at the greatest distance from the earth,
being unmixed, undefiled, and pure from all nature admitting
of corruption and of death; but the souls of men here below,
enveloped in bodies and passions, have no participation in the
Deity, except as far as lies in grasping Him by conception,
like an indistinct dream, by means of philosophy."[21] Yet men
"long for that Beauty which can neither be spoken nor described—for which the old legend makes Isis desire, seek after,

[17] *Ibid.,* p. 27.
[18] *Ibid.,* pp. 49-50.   [20] *Ibid.,* pp. 35-36.
[19] *Ibid.,* p. 39.   [21] *Ibid.,* p. 68.

and dwell with, and fills things here below, whatever partakes
of birth, with all things beautiful and good. . . ."[22]

Isis, then, is both the creative mother of living things and
the inspirer in the souls of men of the desire for philosophy
and for beauty so that to men "when they are loosed from
the body, and removed into the unseen, invisible, impassible,
and pure region, this God is then their leader and king."[23]
Isis in this aspect of her godhead is identical with Minerva
as Plutarch himself elsewhere remarks: "And the shrine of
Minerva at Sais (whom they consider the same with Isis)
bears this inscription, 'I am all that hath been, and is, and shall
be; and my veil no mortal has hitherto raised."[24]

Diana also is identical with Isis. "Diana of the Ephesians.
. . . This deity originally symbolized Earth, and was actually
identified with Isis; but in later times, being called by the
name of the Grecian Artemis, she similarly became the Pres-
ident of the Moon."[25] The seeming confusion of these iden-
tities is somewhat cleared when the underlying metaphysics
is understood. In the triune nature of man, body is born of
earth, soul of the moon, and mind of the sun. Isis, or soul, is
thus mediator between the earthly man and divine mind to
which he aspires. When man dies to the body it is the earthly
Hermes who "separates the soul from the body, hastily and
with violence; but Persephone gently and slowly loosens the
mind from the soul."[26] And again: "The nature of the soul
is left behind in the moon, retaining vestiges as it were and
dreams of life; and on this account you must suppose it rightly
said:

" 'Like to a dream, the soul took wing and fled.' "[27]

[22] *Ibid.*
[23] *Plutarch's Morals* (trans. by W. W. Goodwin), IV, 136.
[24] *Plutarch's Morals,* King, p. 8.
[25] *Ibid.,* Prefatory note, p. xi.
[26] *Ibid.,* p. 251.   [27] *Ibid.,* p. 255.

Isis, Diana, Minerva—the names but stress varying aspects of the moon goddess whose nature "is not simple and un-mixed, but as it were a combination of star and earth."[28] In this, according to the Platonic philosophy, she is a symbol of the mixed character of the soul, which in its lower aspect is of earth but in its divine aspiration is intellectual, a spark of the eternal mind to which ultimately it returns. Isis, the creative mother, nurses in man this divine aspiration. She is then Minerva, goddess of wisdom. In her earthly creative aspect she is Venus, goddess of love. Her aspects are many, often confusing, for though she is goddess of love and gen-eration, "by means of a perpetually sober life, by abstinence from many kinds of food and from venery, she checks intem-perance and love of pleasure, accustoming people to endure her service with bowels not enervated by luxury, but hardy and vigorous; the object of all which is the *knowledge* of the First, the Supreme, and the Intelligible; whom the goddess exhorts you to seek after, for he is both by her side, and united with her."[29] She is the "Female Principle of Na-ture," "Nurse," and "All-receiving," "The one of numberless names."[30]

Plutarch most admirably initiates the student into this two-fold rationalization of myth. On their physical sides the gods are but names for the forces of nature, exhibiting sun and moon and all celestial phenomena in their relation to the sea-sons and to man dependent upon the beneficence of the heavens for the fruit of the earth. Yet the gods are manifestly easy symbols also for the contest of good and evil, not only in its physical but also its spiritual phases. Sun and moon wage war on darkness and destruction, Typhon. In the mixed na-ture of man, desiring both sensual and spiritual things, mind,

[28] *Ibid.*, p. 253.
[29] *Ibid.*, p. 2.   [30] *Ibid.*, p. 46.

which desires to contemplate good, is forever at war with the body, which clings to earth and the seductions of sense. The elaboration of this philosophy in all its subtleties and complications will appear in an examination of certain of the neo-Platonists. Plutarch anticipates their doctrines, and a study of his thought makes his successors more easily intelligible.

Likewise in Plutarch, besides the physical and metaphysical rationalization of the Greek and Egyptian myths, is apparent the often bewildering metamorphoses or hypostases of the gods. Thus Juno is also Ceres and Venus and Diana and Persephone and Minerva, according as she is thought of as one or as triune and with manifold names. At the outset this fluidity of nomenclature is perplexing. With familiarity, its convenience as a device for poetic symbolization becomes more evident, and its later adaptation by Shelley intelligible.

MACROBIUS

Macrobius need detain us but briefly after the somewhat full discussion of Plutarch. In him likewise appears the dual interpretation of myth. In its physical aspects the fable of the Greek and Egyptian gods symbolizes the progress of the seasons, the retreat and return of the sun. Isis and Osiris, Venus and Adonis, Castor and Pollux, the identification of Jupiter with Dionysus, the sun-god—all are part of this poetic rendering of natural phenomena. The sun in winter retreats to the Southern hemisphere symbolized by Proserpine; in spring returns to the hemisphere symbolized by Venus. It is said that "the divine or ethereal bodies of the stars are endowed with mind, but are not themselves minds."[31] There are in all nine spheres, the innermost that of the earth, the outermost that of the fixed stars. Each contributes its note

[31] *Macrobius, or Philosophy, Science, and Letters in the Year 400*, by Thomas Whittaker, p. 66.

to the divine harmony which is due to the numerical proportions of the motions one to another. "Since the soul of the world was composed on the basis of musical proportions, it must express itself by causing motions that give rise to audible music."[32] Jupiter he interprets "not as the highest God but as the heaven, and Juno as the air."[33]

Macrobius laments the ruin of the old Egyptian religion and civilization and makes a pantheistic defense of visible beauty. "The oracular Hermes or Thoth, declaring that nature creates by a kind of imagination, glorifies the world and man; makes man in this respect superior to the gods, that he has two sources, the intellectual and the animal or sensitive; affirms that divinity, if terms of sex are applied to it, must be called bisexual, and deifies both male and female in man. . . . Man is expressly celebrated as making the gods in his own image when he imposes his ideal of beautiful form on statues."[34] Macrobius it is evident is partly influenced by the neo-Platonists.

Whittaker's comment anticipates a later perplexity in the interpretation of Shelley, the reconciliation of Minerva with Aphrodite: "However ascetic the neo-Platonists might be personally; however, in their theoretical philosophy, they might place the stability of the life of intellect above the flux of birth; they were careful not to blaspheme sex. For it was part of their view that the world-process must always go on. Thus Julian, whose personal chastity is denied by no one, takes occasion to glorify Aphrodite as sharing in productive power with the Sun."[35] Interesting too is the interpretation of Pan. "The more penetrating, Praetextatus continues [in the *Saturnalia*], will find in Pan, who is called Inuus, not the lord of the woodlands, but the sun as ruler of all material

---

[32] *Ibid.*, p. 73.
[33] *Ibid.*, p. 69.
[34] *Ibid.*, p. 9.
[35] *Ibid.*, p. 26.

substance. This is the real meaning of the name by which
the Arcadians worship him. Of this matter, the force of all
bodies, whether divine or earthly, forms the essence. His
love is Echo, beheld by no eye, but signifying the harmony of
the heavens."[36]

In Plutarch and in Macrobius the influence of neo-Platonism is evident. The gods and their activities are interpreted
as symbols of intellectual truths; mythology is but philosophy
incarnate. Neo-Platonic philosophers pushed this reading of
myth to great lengths, but it is needless in this place to review
their findings. For the convenience of those who wish to go
more fully into the question I have summarized in appendices the conclusions of Cudworth and Thomas Taylor, two
of the most notable English neo-Platonists, insofar as these
conclusions bear upon an interpretation of the *Witch of Atlas*.
It is known that Shelley had some acquaintance with the
works of Taylor. That he had read Cudworth we have no
evidence. But Cudworth is the clearer writer and his rationalization of Greek myth in terms of neo-Platonism one of the
best.

The neo-Platonists, while accepting the physical implications of myth, stress largely the metaphysical. Yet in physical
terms the natural forces personified by the gods and goddesses admitted of greater refinements of definition as science
pushed its discoveries in chemistry, electricity, and meteorology. Thus in the letters of the eighteenth century traveller
Savary the seasonal phenomena of Egypt are explained in a
more modern meteorology than that of Macrobius and Plutarch. Erasmus Darwin, pursuing a hint in the works of
Francis Bacon, rationalizes the ancient myths in terms of the
new chemistry of Lavoisier. The chemistry and meteorology
of the late eighteenth century set all the interrelated phe-

[36] *Ibid.*, p. 29.

nomena of vegetation, rainfall, and electricity in a wholly new light. Perhaps some of this science had been known in ancient times and the knowledge concealed from the vulgar in the guise of myth and symbol. So Darwin reasoned. His speculations, therefore, and parts of Savary's letters I have likewise included in the appendices for the edification of the curious. What is essential to the proof of points of interpretation in the *Witch of Atlas* I cite from these writers, Cudworth, Taylor, Savary, and Darwin as occasion demands. Readers who deem the proofs insufficient may, like the merely curious, find the summaries given in the appendices a convenience.

Shelley, in the *Witch of Atlas,* it is clear upon examination of the poem, employs his mythology in a two-fold way. The Witch and the phenomena which surround her are to be interpreted both in terms of metaphysics and science. Shelley in this dual symbolism is thus pursuing the two paths of interpretation which have been indicated. He however reconciles science and metaphysics with an exactness and fullness not hitherto known and his science—meteorology in chief—is of his own day. He is acquainted not only with the chemistry of Lavoisier but with the work of Beccaria on atmospheric electricity. The Witch, then, identifiable as a goddess of the classical mythology, and her spiritual powers explicable in terms of neo-Platonism, likewise controls natural forces whose activities are in accord with the science which Shelley knew. In the interpretation of the poem this dual reading in physical and in metaphysical terms must be kept constantly in mind. Perhaps the briefest of summaries will make clear the Witch's two-fold activities as spiritual guide and healer and as goddess of natural forces.

Born of Apollo and a sea nymph she is exceedingly lovely, taming all savage beasts, making her influence felt upon universal Pan and the lesser sylvan deities. So beautiful is she and her fascination so great that she must needs veil herself before them in a garment spun of "fleecy mists" and "long lines of light." In the cave in which she lives are magic treasures, sounds, visions, odors, and liquors which "could medicine the sick soul." There are scrolls, also, full of wisdom concerning man and nature.

In the solitude "of this wild home" her thoughts clothe themselves with "the ocean foam," "the wind," or "the speed of fire" to work her bidding. She is the minister of her "mighty sire" in employing the forces he has created. She studies the "scrolls of dread antiquity." She does not sleep but lies at night "in trance within the fountain" or in times of savage weather seeks a well of crimson fire wherein she lies secure. Upon her fountain she has a magic boat propelled by a swift and beautiful creature of her making, Hermaphroditus. The two explore the mountain cataracts, the boat oared by the enchanted wings of Hermaphroditus.

In the interlunar night the Witch betakes herself to "Austral waters" where she finds a windless haven and where her ministering spirits build her a pavilion "of the intertexture of the atmosphere," a pavilion spun of mists and lightnings. There upon her throne she listens to the news brought to her by her agents of all passing between the earth and moon. And again she ascends to the streams of upper air and follows the lightning's track.

Her choicest sport, however, is at night to "glide adown old Nilus" and observe mortals in their sleep. Beneath the unhappiness of mortals, beneath "the liquid surface of man's life" she perceives the secret beauty of souls. To her they are living spirits whether sleeping or in seeming death. And to the souls of men whether in the sleep of life or of death she can bring soothing dreams so that they are happy. To the most beautiful souls she gives "strange panacea in a crystal bowl." Thereafter they live as if controlled by some spirit mightier than life, and death to them has no reality.

Upon the less beautiful souls she imposes dreams wherein the miser, the priest, the king, and the warrior perceive the absurdity of their pursuits. Shy lovers realize in dreams the fulfillment of their love. And friends who have been parted by malice she thus reunites. These are the pranks she plays upon mortal men.

Her activities thus coldly summarized are, it is to be seen, of two kinds, physical and spiritual. It remains, in the examination of the poem, to analyze them in terms of science and metaphysics, to identify the Witch, and learn how, in Shelley's conception of her, these manifold activities are reconciled one with another. The rationalization of myth which is found in neo-Platonism points the way of our approach.

CHAPTER III

THE MEANING OF THE *WITCH OF ATLAS*

T<small>HERE</small> are certain things which it is well to remember before taking up the detailed examination of the *Witch of Atlas* in the effort to decipher its meaning. The poem was very quickly composed in the summer of 1820, a few months after the completion of the fourth act of *Prometheus* and at the very time of the publication of that poem. It is thus a product of the same period of poetic creation as *Prometheus* and the *Cloud*. This fact and the similarities in subject matter and symbol to be found among the three suggest that they were carved from the same block. I believe that the *Cloud* and the *Witch of Atlas* were fashioned from poetic materials rejected in the shaping of *Prometheus,* rejected not because they were inferior but because they did not suit the theme and scope of that grave and profound poem. But the fancies which are spun in the *Witch of Atlas* could not have been evoked from the blue in three days. It is sufficiently remarkable that the actual composition should have been done in so short a time. The fancies, the speculations, the skilled and familiar use of symbols—these are the product of meditation and of time. They came from the same workshop as the *Prometheus*.

Any reader of Shelley will remark the consistency of his ideas and their repeated employment from the relatively unskilled *Queen Mab* to the consummate *Prometheus*. Shelley grows greatly in poetic skill in the ten or twelve years of his creative life, but the ideas and beliefs of his youth remain the preoccupations of his maturity. *Queen Mab, The Revolt of Islam,* and *Prometheus* are three versions of his philosophy, three social and moral homilies poured into the indifferent ears of mankind. The crudities of *Queen Mab* are not to be

found in *Prometheus* but in both is the impassioned dream
of a regenerate world.

Likewise in Shelley's poems recurs even more persistently
his dream of a perfect union with light, or love, or with intellectual beauty. The symbol is usually a woman. In the
Hymn to Intellectual Beauty the vision of loveliness remains
unembodied; but in *Queen Mab* it is the Fairy; in *Alastor* it is
the "veilèd maid" whose beauty intoxicates and haunts the
poet; in the *Sensitive Plant* it is the lady of the garden; in
Epipsychidion it is Emilia Viviani, transitory symbol of divine
beauty; and in *Prometheus* it is Asia, spirit of love and beauty
in Nature, the earthly Venus who is to be united with the
spirit of man.

Shelley's preoccupation with this theme, this symbol, is
suggestive of two things: his dissatisfaction with his earthly
loves, the inadequacy and incompleteness of his marriages
both with Harriet and with Mary; and his ever unsatisfied
search for beauty, for that spiritual completeness of which he
had read in mystical literature and which he had experienced
in his own being. The *Hymn to Intellectual Beauty* suggests
that once, at least, he had known the raptures of mystical
union with the spirit of beauty, with the One, with God, a
union which mysticism and religion alike describe as the aim
and reward of the striving soul of man. But if once experienced, seemingly no lesser earthly union can ever wholly
satisfy. Human love and marriage lure with the promise of
this completeness but it is not to be found on earth. Thus
we read of the Platonic affinities, of the incompleteness of the
soul which was once one and is now divided. The hermaphrodite, symbol of unity and perfection, of the harmonizing
of the male and female principles in nature, becomes for
Shelley a recurrent theme. On earth, in man, in nature there
is strife and discord. In love, in beauty, in philosophy lies the

way to unity and rapture. The unrealized dream, and the longing, are symbolized by Shelley in his delineation of beauty in womanly form, in the Lady of the *Sensitive Plant,* and in the Witch of the *Witch of Atlas.*

The citations already made and, in the appendices, the excerpts from the neo-Platonists, extensive and tedious as these may seem, have accustomed the reader to the dualism inherent in such rationalization and make the employment of symbol a familiar practice. Nor need the discussion of the *Witch of Atlas,* after so long an approach, be too heavily garnished with authority and citation. The essential background has been depicted, the symbolic character of the poem intimated, and the dualism of its figures anticipated. Much now need only be discussed, rather than argued, and the implications suggested. For the more difficult and debatable points further quotations from authority must needs be made, but I shall endeavor to make them as few as will suffice.

First, then, the significance of the title: Why "Witch," when her functions more nearly correspond to those of various goddesses defined in Greek and Egyptian mythology? By "Witch" I take it is meant one who works magic, which in the words of Paracelsus "is great hidden wisdom, just as that which is commonly called human wisdom is great folly."[1] The power of magic is based upon faith and "by faith and imagination we can accomplish whatever we desire. The true power of faith overcomes all the spirits of Nature, because it is a spiritual power, and spirit is higher than Nature."[2] The Witch of the poem in her works is a magician of this order, and it is as a wonder worker through the forces of faith, in-

[1] *The Life of Philippus Theophrastus Bombast of Hohenheim, Known by the Name of Paracelsus, and the Substance of his Teachings,* by Franz Hartmann, p. 161.
[2] *Ibid.,* p. 149.

tellect, and imagination that she identifies herself with the metaphysical aspects of deity.

Her home, fittingly, is Atlas, which is of such great height that it was reputed to support the heavens and was, therefore, made the home of the Demiurgus, which in his intellectual aspect is Minerva. Minerva, goddess of the intelligible, dwells at the highest point of earth where it touches the sky, symbolizing the connection of earthly and heavenly things. Atlas, then, is reputedly her home.[3] There is an initial likelihood, therefore, that the Witch dwelling on Atlas is either herself Minerva or is in some way associated with that goddess, the poet desiring in his poem more freedom for his fancy than would be the case were he to name her outright and circumscribe her activities to those warranted by tradition and myth. Either so, or what is equally probable, by the evasion of the name, by the use of the term "Witch" rather than "Goddess," he spins that playful web of mystification which in the last lines of the dedication he challenges the reader to unravel:

> If you unveil my Witch, no priest nor primate
> Can shrive you of that sin,—if sin there be
> In love, when it becomes idolatry.
> —*W. of A.* ll. 46-48.

The birth of the Witch, we are told in the first stanza, was before Error and Truth, born of Change and Time,

> ... had hunted from the earth
> All those bright natures which adorned its prime.
> —*W. of A.* ll. 51-52.

This would imply the Saturnian age, before Time was; the heavenly age of the Intelligible World when Saturn had not been displaced by Jupiter; when, that is, in the metaphysical reading, material forms created in time had not imperfectly

[3] *The Commentaries of Proclus on the Timaeus of Plato* ... (trans. by Thomas Taylor), Vol. I, Bk. I, pp. 144-45; Bk. III, p. 454.

imitated the timeless archetypal ideas. Either so, or as more plausibly appears, her birth is in the golden age at the beginning of earthly creation before the traditional "fall" and the loosing of evil and pain upon the world.

Her dwelling place is a "cavern by a secret fountain." The cavern, by reason of Plato's familiar parable, is one of the best known of mystical symbols. Shelley employs it so frequently here and in *Prometheus* that it is well at the outset to familiarize ourselves with some of its uses. The cave, first, is the image of the world. Thus we read that "Zoroaster . . . consecrated a native orbicular cave, adorned with flowers, and watered with fountains, to the honour of Mithras, the maker and father of all things: this cave being an image or symbol to him of the whole world, which was made by Mithras."[4] Similarly we learn that certain lines of Virgil "afford a beautiful representation of a corporeal nature, of which a cave, defended with a black lake, and dark woods, is an obvious emblem."[5] Plato makes use of the cave as the symbol of mortal life, in which, shut away from the divine world, we see but the shadows of reality cast upon the wall. The loneliness and obscurity of the individual soul is thus symbolized by the cave; and the ascription of caves to the domain of Neptune, god of souls in generation, is therefore consistent, for to "Jupiter indeed is allotted the summits, and the parts which are raised above others, in which also are the allotments of happy souls . . . because they then live under Jupiter, beyond generation. But Neptune is allotted cavities, and cavernous places, with which generation, motion, and the incursion of concussions are conversant. . . . Whence also, of souls them-

[4] Ralph Cudworth, *The True Intellectual System of the Universe*, II, 57. For discussion of Cudworth's interpretation of neo-Platonism see Appendix A.

[5] Thomas Taylor, *The Eleusinian and Bacchic Mysteries*, p. 53. For discussion of Taylor's interpretation of neo-Platonism see Appendix B.

selves, they say that such of them as have not yet proceeded into generation, but abide in the intelligible are Jovian; but that such as are conversant with generation, are arranged under Neptune. . . ."[6]

The cavern then is a symbol of souls living in this world after their descent from the divine world into mortality and before their descent to the realm of Pluto. Water is the symbol of material things, of the world of generation, and Neptune is the god of water. The Witch in her cavern, then, is a goddess of this world of created things and has, as will shortly appear, an appropriate relation to Neptune. Her cavern is of his kingdom and symbolizes a soul shut apart to itself in the individuality and isolation which is characteristic of human life.

But in her cavern the Witch lives "by a secret fountain," a symbol no less frequently employed than the cave and filled with metaphysical implications. "God, who is, and is called the first Cause, is alone the fountain and original of all things."[7] He is also characterized as "one intellectual fountain of all things."[8] We read also of "the fountain of souls, or Juno,—the fountain of virtues, or Minerva— and the fountain of nature, or Diana."[9] These are derivative or lesser fountains, emblems of that original fountain of the One, the "fount of fire" which is "high above aether."[10] The symbol implies illimitability and eternity, a power that flows ceaselessly from a mysterious source.

Of the fount of nature, which is Diana, the moon is the visible symbol. "The moon is the cause of nature to mortals,

[6] *The Six Books of Proclus, the Platonic Successor, on the Theology of Plato* (trans. by Thomas Taylor), II, 34-35.

[7] Cudworth, *op. cit.*, II, 404.

[8] *Ibid.*, p. 344.

[9] Taylor, *Eleusinian and Bacchic Mysteries*, pp. 113-14.

[10] *Proclus on the Theology of Plato*, Taylor, I, Intro., p. xlix.

and the self-revealing image of the fountain of nature."[11]   She is likewise called "the visible statue of fontal nature."[12]   The sun, it is said, "derives his nutriment from the sea, whereas to the Moon the fountain and lacustrine waters send up a sweet and gentle exhalation."[13]   And if to these passages we but add a passage from Plotinus we shall have, I think, all the associations suggested by the symbol of the fountain, together with weighty authority therefor, that we shall hereafter need.   Wisdom and Thought, Plotinus has been saying, withdraw the soul from lower things and lift it to those above: "The soul, then, purified, becomes Idea and Reason, wholly free of body, intellective, entirely of that Divine order from which the Fountain of Beauty rises and all the stream of Beauty.   Hence the soul lifted up to Intelligence is beautiful to all its power. For Intelligence and what things proceed from Intelligence are the soul's beauty—a beauty native to it and not foreign, for only so is it truly soul."[14]

Fountain, it is clear, while its general significance is evident, is a flexible symbol whose particular implications will vary from instance to instance.   Of the Witch, living in her cavern by "a secret fountain," we can say for the moment no more than that she is associated with some stream of divine energy: whether the creative energy of nature, the divine energy of intellect, or that which is but another name for the energy of intellect, the fountain of beauty.   Her more particular associations will appear in the account of her powers and activities.

The mother of the Witch, the poem tells us, "was one of the Atlantides," one of the daughters, that is, of Atlas.   Atlas, symbol of the starry heaven, was father not only of the At-

[11] Taylor, *Eleusinian and Bacchic Mysteries,* p. 113.

[12] *Proclus on the Timaeus,* Taylor, Vol. II, Bk. IV, p. 231.

[13] *Plutarch's Morals,* King, pp. 35-36.

[14] *Plotinus on the Beautiful* (trans. by Stephen MacKenna), p. 22.

lantides, but also of the Hyades[15] and the Hesperides.[16] Because of their common descent "the children of Atlas were styled Peleiadae."[17] Indeed the term Atlantides, loosely used, was a generic term for nymph. "Nymphs were commonly called Atlantides."[18] Which one of innumerable nymphs or of the many daughters of Atlas may be identified as the mother of the Witch is therefore somewhat problematical. It will be most informative, I think, to inquire into the ancestry and activities of the nymph Dione.

Dione, daughter of earth and heaven,[19] and therefore properly a nymph and one of the Atlantides, is "sometimes looked upon as the mother of Venus. . . . She was said to have been the mother of Niobe; and under the name of Pleione, was esteemed the mother of the Peleiades."[20] Her names are variously, Dione, Ideone, and Deïone "whom the poets supposed to have been beloved by Apollo."[21] As the beloved of Apollo or Jupiter, Dione is the mother of the earthly Venus: "There are two Venuses, and therefore two Loves; one the older and without a mother, the daughter of Uranus or heaven, which we call the heavenly Venus; another younger, begotten from Jupiter and Dione, which we call the vulgar Venus."[22] We read again that there were "four of the name of Venus. . . . The third, daughter of Jupiter and Dione, was wife to Vulcan, and mother of Anteros."[23]

It is plausible, amidst the complexities of the old mythology, to identify Dione, mother of Venus, who was begotten of her

[15] M. de Tressan, *Mythology Compared with History* (trans. by H. North), p. 124.

[16] *Ibid.*, p. 122.

[17] Jacob Bryant, *A New System; or, An Analysis of Ancient Mythology,* V, 27.

[18] *Diodorus the Sicilian*, Booth, I, 202.

[19] *Proclus on the Timaeus*, Taylor, Vol. II, Bk. V, p. 324.

[20] Bryant, *op. cit.*, III, 155.

[21] *Ibid.*, p. 187.

[22] Cudworth, *op. cit.*, II, 466.

[23] Tressan, *op. cit.*, pp. 184-85.

by Apollo, as one of the Atlantides. The Witch of Shelley's
poem is tentatively, then, no other than Venus, goddess of
love and beauty in Nature. I believe this to be his meaning,
but to identify the two as one is dependent much more upon
the correspondence of the Witch's activities with those of
Venus than upon similarity or identity of ancestry. The latter
is of minor, though corroborative, importance.

The Witch is daughter of the Sun and a "fair creature,"
one of the Atlantides.

> He kissed her with his beams, and made all golden
> The chamber of grey rock in which she lay.
> —*W. of A.* ll. 62-63.

Clearly the implications of this union of Sun and Water, of
Apollo and a nymph, or of heaven and earth, are twofold.
The symbols are both physical and metaphysical in their im-
port. It is the latter which I shall first consider.

In the neo-Platonic interpretation of myth, Heaven symbolizes intellectuality and Earth materiality. Their union produces this imperfect universe which partakes of the nature of
both. The marriage of Sun and Water, of intellectual light
and matter, is thus set forth in the difficult language of
Proclus: "Hence Orpheus says that the vivific cause [Proser-
pine] of partible natures, while she remained on high, weaving
the order of celestials, was a nymph, as being undefiled; and
in consequence of this connected with Jupiter, and abiding in
her appropriate manners; but that proceeding from her proper
habitation, she left her webs unfinished, was ravished, having
been ravished was married, and being married generated, in
order that she might animate things which have an adventi-
tious life. For the unfinished state of her webs indicates, I
think, that the universe is imperfect or unfinished as far as to
perpetual animals."[24]

[24] *Proclus on the Timaeus,* Taylor, Vol. II, Bk. V, pp. 355-56.

The correspondences of this passage with the passage in the
poem describing the union of the Sun with the Nymph whom
we have tentatively identified with Dione, mother of the
earthly Venus, are sufficiently close. The child of this union
would be one of a mixed nature partaking both of light,
which is intellect, and water, which is the symbol of matter.
Hers would be, then, the domain of soul, which is intermediary between matter and intellect; and her function would
be to create natural forms as nearly in the likeness of their
heavenly archetypes as the imperfect character of matter permits. "For the demiurgus renders the whole world animated,
endued with intellect, and an animal, and constitutes the triple
life which is in it, one indeed being impartible and intellectual, another partible and corporeal, and another between
these, impartible and at the same time partible."[25]

The "lower Venus" or Love, says Cudworth, "is said to
have been begotten from Jupiter himself (the superior soul
of the world) and Dione, a watery nymph."[26] Venus, Diana,
Proserpine—the goddess of Nature so variously named, appears in many guises. As Proserpine she presides "in a leading
and ruling manner over all mundane natures, and as the cause
of only-begotten animals."[27] Venus "is the cause of beauty to
generated natures, which is an imitation of intelligible beauty.
This goddess also is the source of the union of form with
matter; connecting and comprehending the powers of all the
elements; and her principal employment consists in beautifully illuminating the order, harmony, and communion of all
mundane concerns. She likewise governs all the coördinations in the celestial world and the earth, binds them to each

[25] *Proclus on the Theology of Plato,* Taylor, I, 370.
[26] Cudworth, *op. cit.,* III, 94-95.
[27] *Proclus on the Timaeus,* Taylor, Vol. I, Bk. II, p. 386.

other, and perfects their generative progressions through a kindred conjunction."[28]

The intermediary function of the earthly Venus is sufficiently clear: through her creative powers her aim is to raise the souls of men, which are of a mixed nature, being both earthly and divine, to the higher world of the intellect. More of her activities and powers in this metaphysical aspect will appear in the course of this inquiry. It needs now to initiate the discussion of the physical origin of the Witch and the physical and chemical associations which plausibly pertain to her. For the dual aspect of the poem must constantly be borne in mind. The symbols which the poet employs have always their metaphysical and their physical meaning.

The nymph kissed by the beams of the sun is "dissolved away" and "changed into a vapor and then into a cloud." The physical transformations suggest some such chemical union as Darwin believed symbolized in the loves of Jupiter for earthly maidens. In this instance the natural phenomenon is precisely what the poet describes: the creation of water vapor, which again is transformed into a light cloud. The next two stages of the physical evolution of the Nymph who carries within her womb the child of the sun are less obvious. She becomes a meteor such as capers on hill-tops "when the moon is in a fit," and then "one of the mysterious stars" which, the poet says, are invisible but which are "between the Earth and Mars."

The use which Shelley has so clearly made in *Prometheus* of electrical phenomena suggests the answer to the present problem. The element common to the four transformations of the Nymph, the force embodied in each, is electricity. The sun, drawing the water vapor, creates an electric charge with each particle, and the cloud, which is an aggregate of such

[28] *Proclus on the Theology of Plato*, Taylor, II, 143.

particles, has within it the potential lightning. But what connection with electricity have the meteor and the mysterious star? I have elsewhere discussed the matter to some extent in connection with a passage in *Prometheus*.[29] Here I shall briefly restate and amplify the evidence.

Erasmus Darwin, reviewing the electrical theory of his time, believes in a superatmosphere of hydrogen enclosing the air. The two intermixing at the edges and ignited by an electric spark produce the phenomena of fireballs and northern lights.[30] At the next lower level, in the upper thin atmosphere, shooting stars are created, these due to invisible water vapor adhering to particles of air and ignited by electric sparks.[31] In the lower dense atmosphere occurs the common phenomenon of lightning. All of these phenomena are in Darwin's terminology "meteors,"[32] and all are electric in origin. Shelley's own employment of the term "meteor" in various instances suggests a similar loose signification.

I pass over, for the moment, the intriguing allusion to the moon "in a fit" and its possible bearing on the phenomenon of the meteor. The moon and her implications, both physical and metaphysical, will be elaborately discussed later. The immediate concern is with "one of those mysterious stars" and its possible connection with electricity. I shall merely summarize such of the theories of Shelley's time as I am acquainted with. The phenomena of meteorites and falling stones excited much speculation and the literature is evidently large. My own knowledge of it is necessarily slight but perhaps sufficient for the purpose.

A volume by Edward King, *Remarks Concerning Stones,* London, 1796, goes into the whole question of the so-called

[29] *A Newton Among Poets,* pp. 53-55.
[30] *Botanic Garden,* I, Additional Note No. I. For discussion of Darwin's scientific rationalization of myth see Appendix D.
[31] *Ibid.*   [32] *Ibid.*

"thunder stones" often observed to fall in showers. Many instances of these are recorded and the character of the stones is examined and their constitution determined. It is concluded "that the stones were generated in the air, by a combination of mineral substances, which had risen somewhere or other, as exhalations, from the earth."[33] These exhalations are usually attributed to volcanoes, "ashes, and sand, and pyritical and sulphureous dust, mixed with metallic particles from volcanoes; fit for the instantaneous crystallization and consolidation of such bodies as we have been describing,"[34] and these fused by lightning into stony masses: "Lightning is an electrical stroke on a large scale.—If then the reduction of iron can be obtained, by the discharge of an electrical machine; why should not this be accomplished as well and with greater effect by the powerful discharge of the lightning of the Clouds?"[35] These conclusions were examined by other scientists and were approved by some if not all.[36]

That the place of the moon in Shelley's cosmology is important, and its relation to the earth full of subtleties both physical and metaphysical, is clear alike in *Prometheus* and the *Witch*. The vagaries of the moon's orbit, the inequalities of her attraction for the earth, and the consequent variations in atmospheric and magnetic phenomena due to the phases of the moon, to her seasonal changes, and eclipse—these are the theme for numerous allusions. I have discussed the subject to some extent elsewhere,[37] but wish to stress, for its importance in the *Witch,* a point there but lightly touched. The passages which I cite are from Laplace: "As the gravity at the surface of the Moon, is much less than at the surface of the Earth,

[33] Pp. 7-8.
[34] *Ibid.,* pp. 12-13.   [35] *Ibid.,* p. 24.
[36] Tiberius Cavallo, *Elements of Natural or Experimental Philosophy,* IV, p. 391 *et seq.*
[37] *A Newton Among Poets,* chaps. IX and X.

and as this star has no atmosphere which can oppose a sensible
resistance to the motion of projectiles, we may conceive that
a body projected with a great force, by the explosion of a
lunar volcanoe, may attain and pass the limit, where the attraction of the Earth commences to predominate over that of
the Moon . . . then in place of falling back on the Moon, it
becomes a satellite of the Earth, and describes about it an orbit
more or less elongated. The direction of its primitive impul-
sion may be such as to make it move directly towards the
atmosphere of the earth; or it may not attain it, till after several and even a great number of revolutions, for it is evident
that the action of the Sun, which changes in a sensible manner
the distances of the Moon from the Earth, ought to produce
in the radius vector of a satellite which moves in a very ex-
centrick orbit, much more considerable variations, and thus at
length so diminish the perigean distance of the satellite, as to
make it penetrate our atmosphere." This body, says Laplace,
enflamed by air resistance might detonate and "present to us
all those phenomena which meteoric stones exhibit."[38]

In his Notes to his volume Laplace elaborates on this theory
of the lunar origin of meteorites, showing mathematically that
a lunar volcano would possess sufficient force to project masses
of rock to such a distance that they would not fall again to the
moon. The moon's atmosphere would not retard the course
of such masses. Moreover "the appearances observed in the
moon indicate traces of more powerful and extensive volcanoes
than on the surface of the earth."[39] The lunar origin of
meteorites he considers likely but he concludes: "Besides the
threefold opinion of their origin, given in the text, namely, a
lunar, a volcanic, and atmospheric, some philosophers have

[38] Pierre Simon, Marquis de Laplace, *The System of the World* (trans. by
H. H. Harte), II, 81.
[39] *Ibid.*, p. 429.

supposed that they were small planets, or fragments of planets, like those lately discovered, revolving in space, and which, meeting with the earth's atmosphere, are ignited by the friction which they experience in the earth's atmosphere."[40]

Meteorites, then, whether of atmospheric origin, or projected from the volcanoes of the moon, or, as planetoids encircling the earth, falling upon it at certain times when the gravitational pull of sun and moon permits, are in all interpretations associated either with electric action in the atmosphere and the volcano, or with the moon in her gravitational and magnetic pull upon the earth. The "mysterious stars" which "hide between the earth and Mars" are presumably the planetoids of Laplace's comment. The mother of the Witch, becoming one of these in the last of her metamorphoses, departs from the electrical associations evident in water vapor, cloud, and meteor. Yet there must be some logical sequence in the transition; the "dark stars" must in some way be connected with atmospheric phenomena and the display of electric force. The connection lies in the influence of the moon upon atmospheric phenomena as her magnetic attraction for the earth varies with her phases. In later stanzas this physical relation of moon to earth, no less than her metaphysical relation, will become more evident. Meanwhile it is pertinent to note the celestial origin ascribed in classical mythology to falling stones and meteorites and their identification as sacred stones with the worship of Diana, the moon goddess.

King, revolted at the heathenish practice of the ancients in worshipping stones, tells something of the old associations of the worship of Diana and the meteorites, her symbol: "In the Acts of the holy Apostles, we read, that the chief magistrate, at Ephesus, begun his harangue to the people, by saying, 'Ye men of Ephesus, *what man is there that knoweth not how that*

[40] *Ibid.*, p. 430.

city of the Ephesians is a worshipper of the great goddess Diana, and of the IMAGE *which fell down from Jupiter?'* ... And the learned *Greaves* leads us to conclude this image of Diana to have been nothing but *a conical, or pyramidal stone,* that fell from the clouds. For he tells us, on unquestionable authorities, that many others of the images of heathen deities were merely such.

"Herodian expressly declares, that the Phoenicians had no statue of the sun, polished by hand, to express an image; but only had a certain *great stone, circular below, and ending with a sharpness above, in the figure of a cone, of black colour. And they report it to have fallen from heaven, and to be the image of the sun.*

"So Tacitus says, that at Cyprus, *the image of Venus was not of human shape; but a figure rising continually round, from a larger bottom to a small top, in conical fashion.* And it is to be remarked, that *Maximus Tyrius* (who perhaps was a more accurate mathematician), says, the stone was *pyramidal.*"[41]

King goes on to say: "It is hard to conceive how mankind should ever have been led to so accursed an abomination, as the worship of stocks, and stones, at all: but, as far as anything so horrid is to be accounted for, there is no way so likely of rendering a possible account; as that of concluding, that some of these pyramidal stones, at least, like the image of Diana, actually did fall, in the earliest ages, from the clouds; in the same manner as these pyramidal stones fell, in 1794, in Tuscany."[42] And again we find the worship of these falling stones associated with the worship of the emerald, the stone sacred to Astarte (who is Diana or Venus): "The Colossal emerald of the temple of Melkarth at Tyre is designated in the fragments of Sanchoniathon as ... [a] star fallen from

[41] King, *op. cit.,* pp. 14-15.   [42] *Ibid.,* pp. 15-16.

heaven. It was said to have been raised up by Astarte, and this last myth is represented on the silver coins of Marium in Cyprus. Here the radiance and splendor of the object suggested a stellar or celestial origin, and we see the same tendency at work in the application of the name *cerauniae* (thunderstones) to certain brilliant gems by Pliny."[43]

Here is a most curious body of lore, having to do with atmospheric phenomena which involve electricity; meteors; mysterious stars (which are apparently planetoids or meteorites); falling stones sacred to Diana or Venus; and the love of Jupiter for a nymph which results in the birth of, presumably, the earthly Venus, the creative agent of earthly life. The poem describes her birth:

> . . . in that cave a dewy splendor hidden
>   Took shape and motion; with the living form
>   Of this embodied Power the cave grew warm.
>   A lovely lady garmented in light
>   From her own beauty . . .
>
> —*W. of A.* ll. 78-82.

The physical attributes are heat and light, and the goddess is spoken of as embodied power. We need but recall that fire is the earthly counterpart and symbol of the divine creative fire, and that lightning, in the neo-Platonic symbolism implies fabrication, to perceive that in the account of the birth of Venus Shelley has blent the metaphysical interpretations of philosophy with the physical manifestations of electric energy. One additional but illuminating point: In *Prometheus* Shelley clearly identifies electricity with "love which is as fire" emanating from Asia the earthly Venus.[44] Electricity is the earthly counterpart, or physical symbol of the divine creative fire which is love.

Whatever minor difficulties remain to be ironed out in this

[43] George F. Kunz, *The Magic of Jewels and Charms*, pp. 81-82.
[44] *A Newton Among Poets*, pp. 132-33.

dual interpretation of Shelley's images into terms physical and metaphysical, it can safely be assumed in the ensuing stanzas that Shelley is describing some of the experiences of the earthly Venus in her manifold activities and her various aspects, whether intellectual as Minerva or sensuous as Venus, goddess of procreation. And likewise concurrently with this metaphysical reading of symbol is the physical rendering of myth in terms of meteorology. The ancient myths and their readings by rationalists and metaphysicians often curiously anticipate the findings of later scientists. Thus the use of lightning as the symbol of fabrication becomes profoundly significant in Shelley's age which was beginning to manipulate the wonder-working energy, electricity, and was ascribing to it all manner of attributes, seeing in it the spirit of animation or the mysterious ether which Newton had postulated, the energy which, emanating from God, was creator of all forms of force and of matter. In *Prometheus* Shelley attempts a profound synthesis of the neo-Platonic philosophy and modern science. In the *Witch of Atlas* he is playing with the same body of facts and the same conclusions, and with a slightly ironic mockery challenges the reader to follow and understand him in a flight, seemingly of fancy, but indeed most subtle, consistent, and intellectual.

Of the Witch it is said

> And her low voice was heard like love, and drew
> All living things towards this wonder new.
> —*W. of A.* ll. 87-88.

To her came all creatures, "sanguine beasts her gentle looks made tame," all of which "drank before her at her sacred fount" and beheld her "gentleness and power." She teaches them to "forego their inborn thirst of death," for she it is "that makes them have kindly thoughts and work the works of peace."[45]   She is goddess of earth who "is our nurse, as inspiring our lives from her own proper life."[46]   She is Venus who illuminates "all things with union and harmony."[47]   She is "the cause of beauty to generated natures, which is the imitation of intelligible beauty."[48]   As Proserpine she presides "in a leading and ruling manner over all mundane natures, and as the cause of only-begotten animals."[49]   She is "the most Beautiful *Diana*";[50] and she is Isis, "the *Female Principle of Nature* . . . the one of numberless names."[51]

The "sacred fount" of the goddess is presumably symbolic of the divine love, to drink of which is to forget base earthly passions, for the creatures who do so drink are tamed from their savagery and the pard seeks to become "as gentle as the doe." Shelley here, as often elsewhere, describes the golden age, whether legendary or prophetic, in which the world and all its creatures are ruled by love instead of hate. Presumably in this instance it is the golden age of myth before "error and truth" had expelled from earth the "bright natures which adorned its prime."

The various gods and demi-gods of the woods seeking the "Lady love," find her in a cave "upon a seat of emerald stone." The cave, symbol of earth, of earthly life, of the individual soul, of a secret place associated with oracles and divination, seems in this instance to bear the latter connotation. The forest creatures come to her as to an oracle and, it is twice said, she receives them upon "her emerald throne." The hint is explicit, for the emerald is peculiarly sacred to Venus and it is significant to observe too, in the present instance, that "In

[45] John Burnet, *Early Greek Philosophy*, p. 222.
[46] *Proclus on the Timaeus*, Taylor, Vol. II, Bk. IV, p. 286.
[47] *Ibid.*, Vol. I, Bk. I, p. 66.
[48] *Ibid.*, Vol. II, Bk. IV, p. 228.   [49] *Ibid.*, Vol. I, Bk. II, p. 386.
[50] Whitelocke Bulstrode, *An Essay of Transmigration*, p. 50.
[51] *Plutarch's Morals*, King, p. 46.

some cases, the stone which was held to be a dwelling-place of the divinity was also regarded as a representation, or epitome, of some sacred mountain."[52]

The emerald in its associations and the powers ascribed to it is of considerable interest. "As a symbol of life and generation," it is "connected . . . with the Goddess of Love."[53] Also it is associated with the Moon and "was considered particularly fortunate for women at childbirth, and was held to promote constancy and domestic felicity."[54]   It was believed by the Romans "that nothing evil could remain in the presence of this gem."[55]   Among its manifold powers it was supposed to strengthen memory, restore sight, reveal adultery, and give a knowledge of the future.[56]

"The ancient emeralds," we read, "are now known to have come largely from Upper Egypt."[57]   But the term seems to have been loosely used of various green stones.   Thus to the lizard are ascribed powers identical with those of the emerald and it was held to be "a type of the *Logos,* or 'Divine Wisdom,' and was placed upon the breast of Minerva, as frequently seen on ancient engraved gems."[58]   Theophrastus likewise discusses "bastard emeralds" which were "no more than common crystals tinged by particles of copper dissolved in an acid" and which had no more than "some resemblance, perhaps in some cases in little more than color, to the Gems they had the credit to be named from."[59]   Thus we find in this loose category "the Lapis Lyncurius, which is likewise used for engraving Seals on, and is of a very solid Texture, as

[52] Kunz, *op. cit.,* p. 83.
[53] *Ibid.,* p. 305.
[54] Wm. Thomas and Kate Pavitt, *The Book of Talismans,* p. 181.
[55] *Ibid.*   [57] *Ibid.,* p. 277.
[56] Kunz, *op. cit.,* p. 135.   [58] Pavitt, *op. cit.,* p. 95.
[59] *Theophrastus's History of Stones.   With an English Version. . . .* By John Hill, p. 67.

stones are; it has also an attractive Power, like that of Amber, and it is said to attract not only Straws and small pieces of Sticks, but even Copper and Iron, if they are beaten into thin pieces."[60]

This gem, loosely classified as an emerald, is evidently the tourmaline. "Such is the confusion in the statements made by the early Greek and Latin writers as to the emerald, under which generic name they seem to have included almost all green stones of any ornamental or other value, that we cannot absolutely reject the conjecture that Theophrastus (third century B.C.), the earliest of these writers on precious stones, *might* have referred to specimens of green tourmaline, when he states that the true emerald appeared to have been produced from jasper. . . ."[61] The significance of this statement is that the tourmaline, because of its electric qualities, was the subject of considerable investigation in the latter eighteenth century.[62] It is not unlikely, therefore, that Shelley ascribes to the emerald the electric properties of the tourmaline. I would not unduly press the point, which is of minor importance, yet so full is Shelley's poem of symbol, and so complete are the correspondences of metaphysical with physical properties, that the association of electric power with the emerald as symbolical of the creative power of the earthly Venus is not at all far-fetched.

Whether electric or no, the emerald throne is the throne of the goddess of love and harmony in nature, to whom comes the "universal Pan" who "felt that wondrous lady" and she, also, "felt him." Clearly influencing each other these divine powers are differentiated, however kindred their functions. And such is the profusion of powers ascribed to the gods, their multitudinous names and avatars, that it is only by inference

[60] *Ibid.*, pp. 73-76.
[61] Kunz, *op. cit.*, p. 53.   [62] *Ibid.*, p. 54 *et seq.*

and from the poem itself that we can guess what Shelley had
in mind. We read that Pan is sometimes thought of as no
less than Jupiter, "the disposer of all things and of the whole
world."[63]   Apollo sometimes is identified with Pan.[64]   As
such he is, in the words of Cudworth, "a universal Numen . . .
and . . . plays upon the world as a musical instrument."[65]
Again, "by him the Arcadians and Greeks meant, not the
corporeal world inanimate, nor yet as endued with a senseless
nature only, but as proceeding from an intellectual principle
or Divine spirit, which framed it harmoniously; and as being
still kept in tune, acted and governed by the same. Which
therefore is said to be the universal pastor and shepherd of
all mankind."[66]

"For that the Arcadic Pan was not the corporeal world
alone, but chiefly the intellectual ruler and governor of the
same, appears from this testimony of Macrobius . . . the Arcadians worship this god Pan (as their most ancient and hon-
orable god) calling him the Lord of Hyle, that is, not the
Lord of the woods, but the Lord or dominator over all material substance."[67]   Shelley's epithet of "universal" implies, I
think, that he ascribes to Pan such a domination "over all
material substance," and it is this Arcadic Pan, as distinguished
from the intellectual Pan of a higher aspect of divinity, that
Shelley apparently has in mind, for the entire passage is descriptive of Arcadia with its gods and nymphs, its herdsmen
and mountain maidens, and its "rude kings of pastoral Gar-
amant." Universal Pan, god of all material substance, feels
then the influence of the goddess of love and beauty in nature,
of her who shapes living forms in the likeness of their divine

[63] *Proclus on the Theology of Plato,* Taylor, II, Additional Notes, p. xvi.
[64] *Proclus on the Timaeus,* Taylor, Vol. II, Bk. IV, p. 282.
[65] Cudworth, *op. cit.,* II, 456.
[66] *Ibid.*   [67] *Ibid.,* pp. 176-77.

archetypes. That she, too, should feel the influence of Pan is no more than to say, as the myths themselves symbolize, that in the multiform world, so various and so mutable and yet mysteriously one, all things influence each other: matter influences soul and soul matter; and in soul is that spark of the divine, the intellectual, which serves to link matter with its immaterial prototype. If Shelley means this, it is orthodox neo-Platonism. If less, interpret the passage simply as the influence of love and beauty on the lower forms of life.

So beautiful is the Witch that the world is dimmed thereby and all creatures can contemplate nothing else. Wherefore she spins an aerial vesture and weaves a "subtle veil" as "a shadow for the splendor of her love." The image of the veil whereby exceeding brightness and beauty is made supportable to earthly eyes is a familiar one in Shelley. Most readily recurs the song in *Prometheus,* "Life of Life." Asia burning with celestial fire, the earthly goddess of love becoming in her union with Prometheus, the celestial or Uranian Venus, is even within the veil too bright to be borne. The garment of the Witch is woven of mist, light, and starbeams, the most ethereal symbols of the divine fire; yet even so, sufficient to dim the celestial brightness of the goddess. The passage here and the corresponding passage in *Prometheus* recall various parallels in the ancient mythology. Of Isis and Minerva, who are Venus, or hypostases of her, we read: "According to that other inscription upon an altar dedicated to the goddess Isis . . . 'To thee, who being one, art all things'. . . . In the Deity here described, there is both a veil or outside, and also something hidden and recondite; the sense seeming to be this: I am all that was, is, and shall be; and the whole world is nothing but myself veiled; but my naked and unveiled brightness no mortal could ever yet behold or comprehend."[68]   And to Minerva

[68] *Ibid.,* p. 171.

we read this inscription: *"I am the things that are, that will be, and that have been. No one has ever laid open the garment by which I am concealed. The fruit which I brought forth was the sun."*[69]

The succeeding stanzas XIV-XVI descriptive of the "sounds of air," the "Visions," and the "odors in a kind of aviary," emphasize the supersensuous implications of sense. The sounds are such as arouse in youth feelings which we think will never die; visions bear their burden of bliss to the saints who worship at the shrine of Love; and the loosed odors "stir sweet thoughts or sad, in destined minds." In identifying the Witch of Shelley's conception we should observe that the sphere of her powers as defined in these passages is mid-way between the world of pure intellect and the kingdom of Pan, the world of material things. Her world, in the neo-Platonic terminology, is that of soul, betwixt the worlds of mind and animal body. Mythologically she is identifiable with Diana and Minerva whose home is the upper atmosphere and the moon. This interpretation will aid in the reading of stanzas XVIII and following descriptive of the magic scrolls with which her cave was stored. But there is stanza XVII descriptive of the "liquors clear and sweet" to be previously considered.

The liquors are seemingly of some transcendent, some supersensuous order, "for they medicine the sick soul" and "change eternal death into a night of glorious dreams." And "if men could drink of those clear vials . . . the living were not envied of the dead." Observe in stanza LXIX a repetition of the same idea and the identical imagery:

> . . . she gave
> Strange panacea in a crystal bowl;
> They drank in their deep sleep of that sweet wave,
> And lived thenceforward as if some control,
> Mightier than life, were in them . . .
> —*W. of A.* ll. 593-97.

[69] *Proclus on the Theology of Plato,* Taylor, II, 169.

If anything can be made of this difficult passage it had best be considered as a whole. The repetition of the thought and the imagery suggests no chance flight of fancy but a well based intellectual concept. I shall postpone, therefore, the discussion of stanza XVII to its more appropriate place in conjunction with stanza LXIX.

The scrolls with which the Witch's cave is stored are "works of some Saturnian Archimage." The word Saturnian implies "purely intellectual," the highest order of divinity: "Because, therefore, this God is the leader of all intellectual life, and every intellect as well that which is imparticipable, as that which is participable proceeds from this cause, hence it belongs to this mighty God to feed in a distributed manner, and to nourish souls. For because indeed he is intelligible in intellectuals, he nourishes souls, and souls are called the nurselings of Saturn."[70]   And again: "When the soul falls into the planet Saturn, which Capella compares to a river voluminous, sluggish, and cold, she then first merges herself into fluctuating matter, though purer than that of a sublunary nature, and of which water is an ancient and significant symbol . . . and Saturn, as we have already observed, is *pure* [intuitive] *intellect*."[71]   The Saturnian Archimage is a creative intellect in the highest realm, that of mind, realm of the archetypes whence proceed the forms of the sensible world: "There are, therefore, prior to sensible figures, self-moving, intellectual, and divine reasons of figures. And we are excited, indeed, from the obscurity of sensible forms, but we produce internal reasons, which are the lucid images of others. And we possess a knowledge of sensible figures, by their exemplars resident in soul, but we comprehend by images such as are intellectual and divine."[72]

[70] *Proclus on the Theology of Plato*, Taylor, I, 329.
[71] Taylor, *Eleusinian and Bacchic Mysteries*, p. 165.
[72] *The Philosophical and Mathematical Commentaries of Proclus, on the First Book of Euclid's Elements* (trans. by Thomas Taylor), I, 154.

In the ancient mythology Isis and Minerva symbolize
knowledge: "Isis is a Greek word, which signifies knowledge;
and Typhon is the enemy of this goddess."[73]   Minerva, the
highest offspring of God, is in the neo-Platonic rationalization
of myth "that original, intellectual, ruling, and providential
deity, who guards and preserves all middle lives in an immutable condition, through intelligence and a self-supporting
life, and by this means sustains them from the depredations
and inroads of matter."[74]   Minerva thus, as an hypostasis of
Juno, is the "intellectual part of . . . soul."[75]   She is the "savior
Minerva, by philosophical discipline of mind and heart purifying the nature."[76]   As Neith in the Egyptian mythology,
Minerva is "the divine wisdom which guides the world, and
enlightens men, and . . . the protector of the arts."[77]   Minerva
"is *Calliergos,* or the beautiful fabricator, as connecting by
beauty all the works of the father; a *Virgin,* as exerting an
undefiled and unmingled purity."[78]   She is goddess of the
arts, for by contemplation of the arts the soul is stirred to the
perception of sensuous beauty and thereby to the higher beauty
of mind. "The Beautiful addresses itself chiefly to sight; but
there is beauty of sound, too, both in sequences of words and
in all Music . . . and, to rise from the realm of Sense to a
higher order, there are pursuits, actions, faculties, sciences that
have beauty, and there is the beauty of the virtues. . . . And
this inward vision, what is its operation? Newly awakened,
it is all too weak to gaze upon its brilliant mark. Therefore
the soul itself must be trained to the habit of contemplating,
first, all beautiful pursuits, then works of beauty—not those

[73] Cudworth, *op. cit.,* II, 199.   [74] Taylor, *op. cit.,* p. 199.
[75] *Proclus on the Timaeus,* Taylor, Vol. II, Bk. V, p. 328.
[76] Taylor, *Eleusinian and Bacchic Mysteries,* p. 100.
[77] Claude E. Savary, *Letters on Egypt,* II, 318. For discussion of Savary's
work on rationalization of myth see Appendix C.
[78] *Proclus on the Timaeus,* Taylor, Vol. I, Bk. I, p. 142.

that the arts labour but the actions of men known as good. Lastly, you must observe the souls of those that have shaped these works of beauty. . . .[79]

In the Saturnian scrolls of which Minerva is the interpreter to man are set forth the ideals whereby the world may reattain "that happy age too lightly lost" and "quench the earth-consuming rage of gold and blood." Therein also are the secrets of science whereby men may master

> Time, earth and fire, the ocean and the wind.
> —*W. of A.* l. 196.

The stanzas epitomize the theme of *Prometheus*, which dramatizes the return to the golden age and in its lyric epilogue portrays the universe as directed by the liberated human mind. And to the perfected human mind no longer ruled by hate and fear is revealed "the inmost lore of Love."

The "wondrous works of substances unknown" with which the cave is heaped are made from "blocks of savage stone" as transformed by the power of the sun. Shelley may mean unknown elements and metals produced by the natural processes of nature or artificially made by the operations of fire upon matter. The implication is chemical and recalls a passage in Erasmus Darwin (Appendix D) who perceived in the loves of Jupiter for earthly ladies an allegory of the chemical processes of nature.

The Witch, it is said, "at first lived alone," and in stanza LXVIII we read

> 'Tis said in after times her spirit free
> Knew what love was, and felt itself alone;
> But holy Dian could not chaster be
> Before she stooped to kiss Endymion,
> Than now this lady . . .
> —*W. of A.* ll. 584-88.

[79] *Plotinus on the Beautiful*, MacKenna, pp. 9, 27-28.

If the Witch is to be thought of as Diana or Minerva it is traditionally as a virgin: "And the third [power] is a divine and undefiled intellect, comprehending in one, in a ruling manner, total virtues. Timaeus, therefore, manifests this, calling the third monad (Minerva) philosophic, as being full of intellectual knowledge, and true wisdom; but philopolemic, as the cause of undefiled power, and the inspective guardian of the whole of fortitude. And again, the Athenian guest calls her Core, as being a virgin, and as purifying from all conversion to externals."[80] If later "she knew what love was" it may be that in the terms of myth it was the love of Diana for Endymion or of Venus for Adonis, though the Witch is throughout described in the chaste terms better suited to Minerva and Diana than to Venus. Yet it is not unreasonable to glance at another possible meaning. If indeed the story of the Witch grew from Shelley's imaginings when he conceived the story of *Prometheus,* and if herein he is depicting the youth of Asia, goddess of love and beauty in Nature, the love she knew later was for Prometheus, the mind of man, when, in the Promethean day, man and nature were united.

The Witch in her solitude is a creative power whose thoughts clothe themselves with the ocean-foam, with the wind, and with fire:

> . . . such power her mighty Sire
> Had girt them with, whether to fly or run,
> Through all the regions which he shines upon.
> —*W. of A.* ll. 214-16.

Metaphysically, in the terminology of neo-Platonism, it is mind which shapes in matter the images of its thought. To think is to create; and Minerva is the intellectual aspect of the creative triad which is summed up in Rhea, or Juno, or Ceres. As Minerva this power is mind, as Diana soul, as Proserpine

[80] *Proclus on the Theology of Plato,* Taylor, II, 39.

the vivific power. The names of these divinities and the ascription of their powers vary somewhat in the several rationalizations of myth but the general principle is clear. The creative power of intellect symbolized in the ethereal fire, is in its earthly form the fire of the sun, or electricity, which is created by the sun's fire operating on matter (water). Appropriately therefore the thoughts of the Witch employ the media of electricity

> Clothing themselves, or with the ocean foam,
> Or with the wind, or with the speed of fire,
> To work whatever purposes might come
> Into her mind . . .
> —*W. of A.* ll. 211-14.

This dualism of the physical and the metaphysical, this correspondence of material forms and energies with their intellectual counterparts, runs consistently throughout the neo-Platonic philosophy and should be constantly kept in mind in any reading either of *Prometheus* or the *Witch*.

The stanzas XXII to XXIV which bewail the deaths of Ocean-nymphs and Hamadryades, Oreads and Naiads and the physical changes and destruction of the world wherein these dwell I have seen interpreted as the death of paganism at the advent of Christianity. But the Witch, be it observed, exclaims

> I cannot die as ye must—over me
> Your leaves shall glance—the streams in which ye dwell
> Shall be my paths henceforth, and so—farewell!
> —*W. of A.* ll. 238-40.

Should not the Witch, a pagan divinity, consistently perish at the cold touch of Christian philosophy no less than her creatures of the woods and streams? So inconsistent a reading is uncalled for. In ancient myth and philosophy, with its insistence upon mutation and change, is sufficient warrant for earthly decay, though the eternal principles of which the Witch

is symbol and personification endure. Rhea, goddess of creation, "is a certain flux."[81] The soul in its transmigration pursues a round of eternal change, "the Egyptians . . . supposing
this revolution or apocatastasis of souls to be made in no less
space than that of three thousand years."[82] The material
world exists in time and "Time is but an image of that unmade duration, which we call eternity."[83] Even the stars do
not live forever: "their empire had a beginning, therefore is
not eternal."[84] The universe, though in the neo-Platonic
philosophy the intellectual divinities exist forever, is forever
being destroyed and recreated: "For the Stoic, the destruction
of the human race at the end of each cataclysm or world-
conflagration is absolute."[85] As to the fate of man and the
human soul, the ancient philosophies differ; but that there is
throughout the universe a cycle of creation and decay is, so
far as I have read, a belief common to all mythologies and
ancient religions.

The Lady lamenting the evanescence of earthly forms,
weeps—

> . . . the dark and azure well
> Sparkled beneath the shower of her bright tears.
> —*W. of A.* ll. 241-42.

Fountains, as I have said, are among the most frequent of the
symbols employed in the neo-Platonic philosophy. We read
of the "fountain of souls, or Juno,—the fountain of virtues,
or Minerva—and the fountain of nature, or Diana."[86] God,
the spiritual source, is a fount of fire. Of the associated colors, in the Rosicrucian symbolism, red, orange, and yellow
imply fire in one or another of its stages; green (associated
with the emerald and Venus) implies living forms in matter;

[81] *Ibid.,* I, 335.
[82] Cudworth, *op. cit.,* II, 112.
[83] *Ibid.,* p. 278.
[84] Savary, *op. cit.,* II, 314.
[85] *Macrobius,* Whittaker, pp. 75-76.
[86] Taylor, *Eleusinian and Bacchic Mysteries,* pp. 113-14.

blue (associated with the sapphire and Jupiter), implies pure elemental matter, as the sky.[87] "There are only two original colors, red and blue, representing 'spirit' and 'matter.' "[88] If this symbolism holds in Shelley's employment of "dark and azure" wells and wells of fire, the allusion here is to the fount of elemental matter (water) from which all things are shaped in the likeness of the divine archetypes.

The "cavern's fountain-lighted roof" embodies a symbolism now familiar. Therein the Wizard Lady spells out "scrolls of dread antiquity" or she embroiders "some high tale upon her growing woof." The "dread antiquity" I suppose to be synonymous with the Saturnian Age, and the scrolls to contain those images and thoughts which she weaves into the woof of earthly creation, the embodiment of the archetypal forms. But to these intellectual patterns it is said she adds "some grace to the wrought poesy." In that line the poet, not the neo-Platonist, speaks. To the neo-Platonist all earthly forms are less beautiful than their heavenly counterparts, and are but imperfect reminders of the divine. But to the lover of earth it may seem that the goddess adds to her creations a color and a warmth, a human love which enhances the beauty of the intellectual pattern. Shelley's poem itself does precisely that, endowing the chill abstractions of philosophy with warmth and grace, clothing ideas in sensuous imagery.

Stanza XXVII, descriptive of fire and its beauty, is reminiscent of Plotinus: "The beauty in colour, too, is simple, deriving from shape, from the conquest of the darkness in Matter by the appearance of light, the unembodied, which is Reason and Forming-Idea. Hence it is that Fire, unlike all material things, is beautiful in and by itself alone, holding the rank of Form to the other elements, living aloft, . . . itself alone ad-

[87] Hargrave Jennings, *The Rosicrucians, Their Rites and Mysteries,* I, 222.
[88] *Ibid.,* p. 220.

mitting no other to itself, all the others penetrated by it. For
they take warmth, but it does not grow cold; it has colour
primally, they receive colour from it as their Form; therefore
it shines and glows, as it were, by right of being Form. . . .
And harmonies unheard in sound create the harmonies we
hear, and so bring the soul to the consciousness of Beauty,
showing it the one Beauty in another kind. . . . Thus much
of the beauties of the realm of Sense, images . . . and shadows,
fugitives that have entered into Matter—but to adorn and to
ravish where they appear."[89] Of fire itself there are no less
than three forms after the triune concept which is all pervasive in neo-Platonism: "That fire which is truly so, and
which is pure light, exists in the heavens. You must not
however wonder, if most attentuated, and most pure fire, is
in the summits of the air, just as the most gross and turbid
fire, is in the bosom of the earth."[90] The woof which the
Witch held "that dimmed the burning brand" must be of the
second order, that fire which is "in the summits of the air,"
symbol of the creative energy of nature, the lightning or
atmospheric electricity. And the Witch, then, as fabricator,
is Diana, the second hypostasis of Juno (Rhea, Ceres, Venus),
whose habitation is the upper atmosphere and whose celestial
symbol is the moon.

The Lady does not sleep but lies all night in trance "within
the fountain," upon which the "emerald crags" cast their
green shadow. This would seem to be "the fountain of nature
or Diana," for the colour note is green, symbolic of the earthly
aspect of Venus. And the physical energy which is the earthly
symbol, or agent of fabrication, lies quiescent, no longer active.
The passage is in accord with that curious employment of
meteorological lore which is to be found in *Prometheus Un-*

bound and which I need not here reargue. Demonstrably Shelley therein set forth the findings of Beccaria as to the activities of atmospheric electricity in its round.[91] In the daytime it is drawn from the earth by the sun; at night it descends from the air, borne by the dew, and is reabsorbed by the earth. In stormy weather it is dissipated by the wind, and also it is drawn to earth in the lightning. So, in its physical aspects, I read the symbolism of the trance and the descent of the Witch from the "high pinnacles" to the secure place where is the inextinguishable "well of crimson fire," the reservoir of energy within the earth.[92] For it was a theory of Shelley's day, one which he poetically employs in *Prometheus,* that electricity is generated by the earth in its rotation. Of the relation of this electricity to magnetism, and of its circulation from pole to pole, I shall shortly have more to say. That the earth is a reservoir of electric energy a couplet from Darwin will suffice (for poetical purposes) to demonstrate:

> From earth's deep wastes *electric* torrents pour,
> Or shed from heaven the scintillating shower.
> —*Botanic Garden,* I, ll. 463-64.

I have assumed in this argument and have, I believe, already shown, that Shelley's rationalization of myth is done both in physical and metaphysical terms, and that in his meteorology he has expanded upon and interpreted in terms of a more modern science the ancient sun myth of Egypt and Greece. The relationship of the Witch to the Moon is elaborately symbolized in subsequent stanzas. If, however, I may, for the moment, anticipate the difficult discussion which these involve, I should point out the analogy of the Witch's withdrawal, in winter, to the fount of fire, in which she dwells secure, to the myth of the sun's withdrawal to the

[91] See *A Newton Among Poets,* chap. VIII.
[92] *Ibid.,* chap. IX.

southern hemisphere in winter and the part played by Isis, the moon, in this yearly round. We read in Savary[93] that "philosophers . . . by Night, Athor, and Venus, meant that season when the sun, having passed the equator, remains in the austral hemisphere; the days then being shorter, and the nights longer." Savary then cites Macrobius to the effect that the upper hemisphere is identified with Venus, and the lower with Proserpine. Venus is represented as in tears when the sun, entering the austral hemisphere, is for a time dead, being detained by Proserpine. Isis (as Butis) in the myth is portrayed as the conserver of the infant Horus, who is the sun waxing in strength on his return from the south.[94] She preserves the infant sun from the attacks of the evil principle, Typhon. The myths are complicated and the metamorphoses of the gods bewildering, but the rôle of Isis, the Moon, is clearly that of the preserver of the sun who is the source of light and energy. Likewise the Witch in her withdrawal from the wintry storms to the well of fire is seemingly the guardian and conserver of energy. But more of this subsequently.

In the ancient myths and philosophies water seems invariably to symbolize matter, its fluidity presumably suggesting the protean forms of things and the eternal flux of the material world. A ship therefore is the recognized symbol, in myth, of the vehicle of the gods, and in philosophy the vehicle of the individual soul, whether human or divine. The implications of the boat and the one directing it are thus expounded by a modern annotater of Porphyry: "The one 'sailing in a Boat' sets before the mind the power that directs the world. As, therefore, the Pilot, being apart from the ship, has the control of its rudders, so the sun subsisting separately has control of the helms of all the world. And as the pilot from

---

[93] *Op. cit.,* II, 307.   [94] *Ibid.,* pp. 379-80.

above at the stern, giving forth from himself the first brief beginning of the course, directs everything, so by an infinite priority of rank, the God from above, imparts without division from the first principles of Nature, the first-operative causes of motions. These things, therefore, and still more than these, are denoted by One Sailing in a boat."[95]

The boat of the Witch "some say Vulcan wrought for Venus," but this proving too feeble for "the ardors in that sphere," "Apollo bought and gave it to this daughter." The poet could hardly be more explicit in declaring the Witch to be the earthly Venus, shadow of the celestial Love. In the world of nature the Witch is the counterpart of the creative Love which exists in the divine, the intellectual sphere. I need not further discuss this familiar dualism. Alternatively the boat is fashioned from a gourd, whose seed was planted by the first-born love. The passage of two stanzas is prettily elaborated. The seed planted by love and producing the magic gourd suggests a fable appropriate to Ceres or to the earth goddess of some Oriental mythology. Ceres is but another name for Venus, the creative principle. The particular fable Shelley may have had in mind I have not identified.

In the several ensuing stanzas the poet elaborates the symbolism of the boat and the force animating it in terms easily intelligible. The boat is moored on the fount, which is the symbol of creative energy; a living spirit is lit within it, and it is endowed with the soul of swiftness. It lies upon the fountain like "a swift flame" on the sceptre of Vesta—symbol of creative energy to the goddess who is identifiable with Juno, Ceres, and Venus. The boat therefore is animated and propelled by one of the three forms of fire, and inasmuch as it is the vehicle of the creative earthly goddess the presumption is

---

[95] Iamblichos. *Theurgia; or, The Egyptian Mysteries* (trans. by Alexander Wilder), p. 241.

that the force is that sublunary fire, the fire of the upper atmosphere, electricity, which is the symbol of Diana.

That this is unmistakably the case is evident in the account
of the creation of the Hermaphrodite, fashioned of "fire and
snow," "the repugnant mass" being tempered with "liquid
love." The "liquid love" is electricity. In a discussion of
Shelley's science in *Prometheus*[96] the identification of love, as
a physical force, with electricity was established. The Spirit of
the Earth draws "love which is as fire" from Asia, the creative
force in nature. In the passage descriptive of the moon and
its energies, moreover, the force emanating from the moon is
characterized as "liquid darkness,"[97] which I have thought
identical with the dark rays of Herschel's discovery. The
similarity of the phrase "liquid darkness" as descriptive of
fluid energy with the "liquid love" and the further identification of "love," as a physical force, with electricity establishes
the meaning of "liquid love." But why the curious fusion of
fire and snow?

The fire and snow, heat and cold, antithetical forces of
expansion and repulsion fused in one force symbolized in the
Hermaphrodite, ask for their interpretation a brief excursion
into the speculations relative to the nature of force, and, in
particular, the force of electricity. From the time of Newton
with his demonstration of the laws of gravity and with his
speculations as to the luminiferous ether and its several manifestations in the force of gravitation, in light, heat, electricity,
and magnetism, to Erasmus Darwin and Davy, the effort of
natural philosophy is to determine some single and unifying
principle of which the various and antithetical forces of nature are the diverse expression. Newton's speculations I have
elsewhere discussed and need not recapitulate."[98] It will suf-

[96] *A Newton Among Poets*, pp. 132-33.
[97] *Prometheus Unbound*, Act IV, l. 226.
[98] *A Newton Among Poets*, chap. VI.

fice to make a few citations from Erasmus Darwin and Cavallo to bring out the significance of the Hermaphrodite as a symbol of the union of attractive and repellant force, of the male and female principles in nature.

The excerpts from Darwin I shall cite without running comment. Observe the effort to establish the similarities of gravity, electricity, and magnetism in their dual character of attractive and repulsive forces:

The power of attraction may be divided into general attraction, which is called gravity; and into particular attraction, which is termed chemical affinity. As nothing can act where it does not exist, the power of gravity must be conceived as extending from the sun to the planets, occupying that immense space; and may therefore be considered as an ethereal fluid, though not cognizable by our senses like heat, light, and electricity.

Particular attraction, or chemical affinity, must likewise occupy the spaces between the particles of matter which they cause to approach each other. The power of gravity may therefore be called the general attractive ether, and the matter of heat may be called the general repulsive ether; which constitute the two great agents in the changes of inanimate matter.[99]

It is the opinion of some philosophers, that the electric ether consists of two kinds of fluids diffused together or combined; which are commonly known by the terms of positive and negative electricity, but are by these electricians called vitreous and resinous electricity. . . .

The magnetic ether may also be supposed to consist of two fluids, one of which attracts the needle, and the other repels it; and, perhaps, chemical affinities, and gravitation itself, may consist of two kinds of ether surrounding the particles of bodies, and may thence attract at one distance and repel at another; as appears when two insulated electrised balls are approached to each other, or when two small globules of mercury are pressed together.[100]

The whole mixed mass of matter of which the earth is composed, we suppose to be surrounded and penetrated by the two ethers, but with a greater proportion of the masculine ether than

[99] Erasmus Darwin, *The Temple of Nature, or, The Origin of Society*, p. 21, note.

[100] *Ibid.*, p. 85, note.

of the feminine. When a stone is elevated above the surface of
the earth, we suppose it also to be surrounded with an atmosphere
of the two ethers, but with a greater proportion of the feminine
than of the masculine, and that these ethers adhere strongly by
cohesion both to the earth and to the stone elevated above it.
Now the greater quantity of the masculine ether of the earth
comes in contact with the greater quantity of the feminine ether
of the stone above it; which it powerfully attracts, and at the same
time repels the less quantity of the masculine ether of the stone.
The reciprocal attractions of these two fluids, if not restrained by
counter attractions, bring them together as in chemical combination, and thus they bring together the solid bodies, which they
reciprocally adhere to; if they be not immovable; which solid
bodies, when brought into contact, cohere by their own reciprocal
attractions, and hence the mysterious affair of distant attraction
or gravitation becomes intelligible, and consonant to the chemical
combinations of fluids.[101]

It is probable that this theory of electric and magnetic attractions and repulsions, which so visibly exist in atmospheres round
larger masses of matter, may be applied to explain the invisible
attractions and repulsions of the minute particles of bodies in
chemical combinations and decompositions.[102]

Cavallo, dissenting from any identification "of the electric
and the ethereal fluid," considers it a futile hypothesis for the
reason that the ether is merely a "*hypothetical fluid,* supposed
by different Philosophers to be endued with different properties, and to be an element of several principles. Some suppose
it to be the element of fire itself, others make it the cause of
attraction, others again derive animal spirits from it."[103] As
to this last speculation a passage from Spallanzani is pertinent:
"But until the principle of life is discovered, which, according
to some, is the union and reciprocal action of the parts in resisting dissolution; or consists in the blood; in a particular
aura, like the imaginary aura seminalis; in something resem-

[101] *Ibid.,* Additional Note XII, sect. xi.
[102] *Ibid.*
[103] Tiberius Cavallo, *A Complete Treatise on Electricity,* I, 121.

bling electricity . . . all reasoning on what affects its creation, preservation, or destruction, must be unsatisfactory."[104]

The air and the forces of air we interpret throughout this inquiry in both physical and metaphysical terms. It is therefore of interest to find in Erasmus Darwin a border-line phenomenon, one which is as easily interpretable in the one as the other. Darwin in the *Botanic Garden* has been describing the function of air in renovating the blood and appends this footnote: "The perpetual necessity of breathing shews, that the material thus acquired is perpetually consuming or escaping, and on that account requires perpetual renovation. Perhaps the spirit of animation itself is thus acquired from the atmosphere, which if it be supposed to be finer or more subtle than the electric matter, could not long be retained in our bodies, and must therefore require perpetual renovation."[105] It is hard to guess whether in this speculation Darwin considers the animating force as physical or metaphysical or whether indeed the distinction has any meaning.

The efforts to ascribe to one force, to a material manifestation of the supposititious ether, phenomena so diverse seemingly as chemical action and the spirit of animation, are evident. To electricity, the most novel and inexplicable of natural forces to speculative scientists of the late eighteenth and early nineteenth centuries, is commonly ascribed the agency of the creative purpose. Shelley's employment of it both in a natural and a supernatural rôle is thus explicable enough. Yet lest anyone believe his identification of force with the spiritual power of love to be without precedent, let me by way of supererogation quote a few lines from Darwin in the invocation to Love in the *Temple of Nature*.

[104] Lazzaro Spallanzani, *Tracts on the Natural History of Animals and Vegetables* (trans. by J. G. Dalyell), I, introductory observations, p. xl.
[105] I, 46, note.

Immortal Love! who ere the morn of Time,
On wings outstretch'd, o'er Chaos hung sublime;
Warm'd into life the bursting egg of Night,
And gave young Nature to admiring Light!—
You! whose wide arms, in soft embraces hurl'd
Round the vast frame, connect the whirling world!
Whether immers'd in day, the Sun your throne,
You gird the planets in your silver zone;
Or warm, descending on ethereal wing,
The Earth's cold bosom with the beams of spring;
Press drop to drop, to atom atom bind,
Link sex to sex, or rivet mind to mind;
Attend my song!

                                            —I, ll. 15-27.

The Hermaphrodite, then, in Shelley's symbolism, is a
natural personification of the two complementary forces of
the world, of attraction and repulsion, of love and hate, for
there are two fluid principles in electricity, the positive and
negative, the resinous and vitreous, the masculine and the
feminine, as they are variously designated.   Yet there is, too,
a mythological background to the Hermaphrodite which
should be briefly sketched, for it is from myth that Shelley
derives this symbol of a force which unifies contrarieties, a
force which in the physical world is a counterpart of the unifying principle of divine love.

That the highest divinities of mythology should be hermaphroditic springs from the nature of their perfection, the
need of their self-sufficiency: "In order ... that we may admire
in a greater degree the conceptions of Plato, we must betake
ourselves to wholes, and to the order of the universe, where
we may survey a wonderful conspiration of the male and female nature.   For in the Gods, indeed, these are so connascent
with each other, that the same divinity is called both male
and female, as is the case with the Sun and Mercury, and
certain other Gods."[106]   In Savary we read, "The Egyptians,

[106] *Proclus on the Timaeus,* Taylor, Vol. I, Bk. I, p. 39.

that they might give the Creator a sensible form, attributed two sexes to him; that is, they acknowledged a power resident in him which could produce without the assistance of any other being. Synesius, full of this ancient theology, speaking of him, says, 'The father, mother, male, and female, art thou.' "[107] The Moon, likewise, is a complete deity: "Thus they place the power of Osiris within the Moon, and say that Isis, being cause of his birth is also his consort. On this account they call the Moon the Mother of Saturn, and hold that she is of hermaphrodite nature."[108] Of the god known as Hermaphroditus it is said he sprang from the union of Hermes and Aphrodite and that he "at some certain times appears to men, and is naturally both man and woman; in beauty and slenderness of his body he represents a woman, but in strength and manly countenance, a man. . . ."[109] And we learn, lastly, from Paracelsus, that "The divine man (the angel) is male and female in one, such as Adam was before the woman became separated from him."[110]

The poet's description of Hermaphroditus is consonant with the ideal of angelic perfection and of beauty, masculine and feminine, blent in one being. Its wings are "tipped" with the speed of "liquid lightnings," a phrase which recalls the "liquid love" of a previous line and other evidences of the poet's identification of love with electric energy. And in the boat of the Lady-Witch it remains asleep until called upon to exert its power and "oar" the boat with "those enchanted wings."

The meaning of the passage is clear enough, but the journey of the Witch through glooms and mountains and hurrying streams invites a word of comment. A stream, in the neo-

[107] *Op. cit.*, II, 312-13.   [108] *Plutarch's Morals*, King, p. 37.
[109] *Diodorus the Sicilian*, Booth, I, 223.
[110] *Paracelsus*, Hartmann, p. 77.

Platonic imagery, is the symbol of the course of human life, of the individual soul making its way to the sea of universal being. A wilderness likewise is the symbol of the individual mind shut in by the bewildering assaults of the senses from the heavenly reality, the divine truths of the intellectual world. Two passages in *Prometheus* employing this imagery should be read in conjunction with the description of the Witch's voyagings. Scene 2 of Act II describes the journey of Asia and Panthea to the cave of Demogorgon. They journey through the dense forest which symbolizes the world of sensation, of sights and sounds which shut away the sight of heaven. Only the dew and an occasional starbeam pierce this wilderness. It is a journey which symbolizes the return of Asia through the experiences of human life to the preëxistence of which Demogorgon is monarch. In scene 5, Act II, Asia sings of this return in her song "My soul is an enchanted boat," concluding with lines which are crowded with neo-Platonic imagery.

> We have passed Age's icy caves,
> And Manhood's dark and tossing waves,
> And Youth's smooth ocean, smiling to betray;
> Beyond the glassy gulfs we flee
> Of shadow-peopled Infancy,
> Through Death and Birth, to a diviner day;
> A paradise of vaulted bowers
> Lit by downward-gazing flowers,
> And watery paths that wind between
> Wildernesses calm and green,
> Peopled by shapes too bright to see,
> And rest, having beheld; somewhat like thee;
> Which walk upon the sea, and chant melodiously!

A detailed examination of this passage is irrelevant here. I would merely point out its evident symbolism and its general likeness to the Witch's journey upon the dark stream amid the mountains. This I assume to imply, metaphysically, the obscure and tumultuous course of individual and earthly existence;[111] and physically to suggest the activities of electricity in the phenomena of earth, stream, and sky, activities which are more explicitly defined in subsequent stanzas. One passage only, prior to stanza XLVII, do I wish especially to discuss, the lines in stanza XLIV descriptive of the "heaven-colored pinions" of Hermaphroditus

> Flinging a glory, like the golden glow
> In which Spring clothes her emerald-wingèd minions,
> All interwoven with fine feathery snow
> And moonlight splendor of intensest rime
> With which frost paints the pines in winter-time.
> —*W. of A.* ll. 396-400.

In lines 219-225 of Act IV in *Prometheus* is a description of the infant, the spirit of the moon, which I have elsewhere discussed in terms of the physical attributes of the moon.[112] The more significant lines are these:

> Within it sits a wingèd infant—white
> Its countenance, like the whiteness of bright snow,
> Its plumes are as feathers of sunny frost,
> Its limbs gleam white, through the wind-flowing folds
> Of its white robe, woof of ethereal pearl,
> Its hair is white, the brightness of white light
> Scattered in strings. . . .

I shall not here repeat the reasons which led me to believe the passage descriptive of electric energy passing through a thin atmosphere or a vacuum. The peculiar phrasing, I hazarded, might be descriptive of some laboratory experiment, one perhaps which passed an electric current through a vacuum tube and produced the effect known as "Canton's Aurora Borealis" as described by Priestley. The conclusions at which I arrived were necessarily tentative, but in the lines in the

[111] See also the poet's journey on the stream in *Alastor*.
[112] *A Newton Among Poets*, p. 150 *et seq.*

Witch is confirmation that they were near the truth, for the description of the light which is flung from the pinions of Hermaphroditus is almost in the same words as these which characterize the spirit of the moon in *Prometheus:*

> Its plumes are as feathers of sunny frost
> —*P. U.* IV, l. 221.

and

> All interwoven with fine feathery snow
> And moonlight splendor of intensest rime.
> —*W. of A.* ll. 399-400.

Evidently the same phenomena are described in both, and that in the *Witch* is unmistakably the radiance of electric energy. Moreover we find in both the association of extreme brightness and coldness and recall the art with which Hermaphroditus was fashioned:

> Then by strange art she kneaded fire and snow
> Together, tempering the repugnant mass
> With liquid love. . . .
> —*W. of A.* ll. 321-23.

The association of extreme brightness and cold, the plumes of "sunny frost" which clothe the moon child and "the fine feathery snow and moonlight splendor" of Hermaphroditus suggest some relationship of moon and electric energy in Shelley's natural and supernatural philosophy. That this difficult problem must be faced and an effort made to solve it is sufficiently evident in stanzas XLVII and XLVIII of the *Witch:*

> Or, when the weary moon was in the wane,
> Or in the noon of interlunar night,
> The Lady-Witch in visions could not chain
> Her spirit; but sailed forth under the light
> Of shooting stars, and bade extend amain
> Its storm-outspeeding wings the Hermaphrodite;
> She to the Austral waters took her way,
> Beyond the fabulous Thamondocana,

Where, like a meadow which no scythe has shaven,
Which rain could never bend, or whirl-blast shake,
With the Antarctic constellations paven,
Canopus and his crew, lay the Austral lake;
There she would build herself a windless haven
Out of the clouds whose moving turrets make
The bastions of the storm, when through the sky
The spirits of the tempest thundered by.

In these and in subsequent stanzas are set forth an array of phenomena with manifold implications. The approach to the problem I believe should be made in this wise: (1) An examination of the relations of moon and earth as interpreted in the neo-Platonic philosophy ; (2) the interpretation of myth in terms of the ancient meteorology—relation of sun and moon to seasons, rainfall, etc.; (3) the reinterpretation of ancient myth in the light of later discoveries in the realm of atmospheric phenomena, electricity, and magnetism. It seems a formidable undertaking, but I shall endeavor to be brief and discuss only those points which have apparent bearing upon the activities of the Witch.

We read in the neo-Platonic philosophy, explaining the triune nature of mind, soul, and body: "First of all, the interior spirit sustains the heaven and earth and watery plains, the illuminated orb of the moon, and the Titanian stars; and the Mind, diffused through all the members, gives energy to the whole frame, and mingles with the vast body [of the universe]. Thence proceed the race of men and beasts, the vital souls of birds and the brutes which the Ocean breeds beneath its smooth surface. In them all is a potency like fire, and a celestial origin as to the rudimentary principles, so far as they are not clogged by noxious bodies. They are deadened by earthly forms and members subject to death; hence they fear and desire, grieve and rejoice; nor do they, thus enclosed in darkness and the gloomy prison, behold the heavenly air."[113]

[113] Taylor, *Eleusinian and Bacchic Mysteries,* p. 98, note.

In the cosmic world the analogies to and origins of the three phases of man are these: ". . . the mind is as much better and more divine than the soul, as the soul is superior to the body. . . . Of these three combined things, the earth furnished for the birth the *body,* the moon the *soul,* the sun the *mind.* . . . The second [death] takes place in the moon, the dominion of Persephone; and of the former the consort is the Earthly Hermes, of the latter, the Heavenly. The former separates the soul from the body, hastily and with violence; but Persephone gently and slowly loosens the mind from the soul. . . ."[114]

The Moon in this trilogy is intermediary between earth and sun, as is the soul of man between body and mind. The Moon therefore is the symbol of soul and is the place from which descend the souls of men: "For Porphyry, placing Minerva in the Moon, says that souls descend from thence, which possess at one and the same time irascibility and mildness."[115] The names of the Moon goddess are legion: she is Rhea, Ceres, Venus, Diana, Hecate, Isis—the goddess of creation in her manifold aspects. Under whatever name, she is a trinity and, as Ceres, is in her various aspects known as Minerva, Diana, and Persephone, according as she is thought of as mind, soul, or body and as dominating these aspects of nature. The citations upon this point could be advanced only too copiously. One will suffice here, as being brief and more intelligible than much of the neo-Platonic writing as translated by Thomas Taylor: "There are, therefore, these three vivific monads, viz., Diana, Proserpine, and our mistress Minerva. And the first of these indeed is the summit of the whole triad, and which also converts to herself the third. But the second is a power vivific of wholes. And the third is a divine

[114] *Plutarch's Morals,* King, p. 251.
[115] *Proclus on the Timaeus,* Taylor, Vol. I, Bk. I, p. 139.

and undefiled intellect, comprehending in one, in a ruling manner, total virtues. Timaeus, therefore, manifests this, calling the third monad (Minerva) philosophic, as being full of intellectual knowledge, and true wisdom; but philopolemic, as the cause of undefiled power, and the inspective guardian of the whole of fortitude. And again, the Athenian guest calls her Core, as being a virgin, and as purifying from all conversion to externals."[116]

Within these theological complications and the obscurities of metaphysics there lies a simple idea: the world of matter, which is a world of flux, aspires to the unchangeable, the eternal; the world of forms emulates the beauty and perfection of the world of ideas; Nature contains within herself the ideal patterns, the matter which she shapes to these, and the aspiration, the desire for perfection, which is the motive force for the creative and evolutionary process. The various phases or hypostases of Isis, the Moon goddess, symbolize these functions. In a sense they are separate but also, in a sense, they are one, as the whole universe in its bewildering multiplicity is one. We read in Plutarch: "The souls of men here below, enveloped in bodies and passions, have no participation in the Deity, except as far as lies in grasping Him by conception, like an indistinct dream, by means of philosophy; but where they are set free and migrate to the Formless, Invisible, Impassive, and Good, then this God becomes leader and king over them, whilst they hang, as it were, upon him, and contemplate without ever being satiated, and long for that Beauty which can neither be spoken nor described—for which the old legend makes Isis desire, seek after, and dwell with, and fills things here below, whatever partake of birth, with all things beautiful and good. . . ."[117]

[116] *Proclus on the Theology of Plato*, Taylor, II, 39.
[117] *Plutarch's Morals*, King, p. 68.

One further passage only, and I shall have done with citation upon the meaning of Isis. It is from Cudworth, eloquently translating and commenting with his customary lucidity: "Behold, here am I, moved by thy prayers, Lucius, that nature, which was the parent of things; the mistress of all the elements; the beginning and original of ages; the sum of all the divine powers; the queen of the seas; the first of the celestial inhabitants; the uniform face of gods and goddesses; which with my becks dispense the luminous heights of the heavens, the wholesome blasts of the sea, and the deplorable silences of hell; whose only divine power the whole world worships and adores, in a multiform manner, and under different rites and names. From which words it is plain, that this goddess Isis was not the mere animated moon (which was rather a symbol of her) but that she was an universal Deity, comprehensive of the whole nature of things; the one supreme God, worshipped by the Pagans under several names, and with different rites."[118]

It is needful in the study of myth and of the neo-Platonic interpretations of myth to be forever alert to the somewhat bewildering nomenclature of the goddess Isis, and to the particular implication which, in varying contexts, any one of her many appellations may bear. Thus as Minerva she is usually to be thought of in her highest, her intellectual aspect, but the name will also be used of her as synonymous with Isis, or as personifying any one of her triune functions. Symbols and names have thus a fluid character which is at first confusing. But for a poet the flexibility inherent in this looseness has its compensations, and it will be found that Shelley both in *Prometheus* and the *Witch* employs his symbols in a fashion which permits a considerable variation, as the context may determine, in the meanings which may be attached to them,

[118] *Op. cit.*, II, 189 (paraphrasing Apuleius).

though the core, so to speak, remains unchanged. Symbols, in short, become a kind of language, and like the words we employ in ordinary speech, vary considerably in their meaning as the context in which they appear alters their values.

From the all too copious literature relating to the Moon as a divinity, and her functions both physical and metaphysical, I shall confine myself to that which has the most obvious bearing upon our immediate problem, the interpretation of the *Witch of Atlas*. And first I should put the statement frequently encountered in neo-Platonic writings, that the "lunar sphere . . . is called by the Egyptians ethereal earth."[119] The meaning of this saying is a little clearer in this form: "For Heaven is in Earth, and Earth in Heaven. And here indeed, Heaven subsists terrestrially, but there Earth celestially. For Orpheus calls the moon celestial Earth."[120] The idea, seemingly, is that the moon symbolizes the soul as intermediary between mind and body, and it therefore partakes both of a divine and of an earthly character: "Souls which derive their subsistence from divinity, but participate of the artificial [or Vulcanic] intellect, are disseminated in the body of the moon; souls that give themselves to the arts, dwelling there; and . . . they have bodies which are effluxions of the ethereal bodies."[121] The lunar sphere embraces, therefore, all sub-celestial things: "The part of the universe that is born and perishes, is surrounded by the Lunar sphere, but all things are set in motion and changed within it by means of the four elements, Fire, Earth, Water, Air. . ."[122] Again: "The Universe (if not the whole, yet that which surrounds Earth, and lies below the Moon), is made inconsistent with itself, and variable and susceptible of frequent changes."[123]

[119] *Proclus on the Timaeus*, Taylor, Vol. I, Bk. I, p. 124.
[120] *Ibid.*, Vol. II, Bk. V, pp. 315-16. [122] *Plutarch's Morals*, King, p. 54.
[121] *Ibid.*, Vol. I, Bk. I, p. 124. [123] *Ibid.*, p. 39.

The Moon, therefore, the residence of souls, is the intermediary between the divine and earthly spheres. As Minerva,
who is intellect and philosophy, she aids in freeing man from
the dream of life: "The nature of the soul is left behind in
the moon, retaining vestiges as it were and dreams of life;
and on this account you must suppose it rightly said:

" 'Like to a dream, the soul took wing and fled.' "[124]

This is the Moon in her celestial aspect, but in her terrestrial
she animates the perishable world: "The motion of the moon
. . . in a various manner changes generation."[125] For "her
nature . . . is not simple and unmixed, but as it were a combination of star and earth; for just as earth mixed with air
and moisture becomes soft, and the blood mingling itself with
the flesh produces sensibility, in like manner they say the moon
being mixed up from her inmost depth, becomes both animated and generative. . . ."[126] As the generative mother the
Moon in her waxings and wanings affects the life of earth:
"The Moon first is arranged in the place about the earth, as
having the relation of nature and a mother to generation. For
all things are convolved by her, are coincreased when she increases, and are diminished when she is diminished."[127]

The Moon, the mother of nature, is, in her rôle of Venus,
"the cause of all harmony, and of the union of the male with
the female, and of form with matter."[128] In her dark phase
"she longs for, and follows after the Sun: for which reason
they invoke the Moon for aid in *love affairs;* and Isis, says
Eudoxus, presides over amours."[129] Yet in another aspect,
"By means of a perpetually sober life, by abstinence from many

[124] *Ibid.,* p. 255.
[125] *Proclus on the Timaeus,* Taylor, Vol. II, Bk. III, p. 3.
[126] *Plutarch's Morals,* King, p. 253.
[127] *Proclus on the Timaeus,* Taylor, Vol. II, Bk. IV, p. 227.
[128] *Ibid.,* Vol. I, Bk. I, p. 29.   [129] *Plutarch's Morals,* King, p. 46.

kinds of food and from venery, she checks intemperance and love of pleasure, accustoming people to endure her service with bowels not enervated by luxury, but hardy and vigorous; the object of which is the *knowledge* of the First, the Supreme, and the Intelligible; whom the goddess exhorts you to seek after, for he is both by her side, and united with her."[130]

Minerva, intellectual aspect of Isis, is the patroness of medicine: "Porphyry . . . says that medicine very properly proceeds from Minerva, because Esculapius is the lunar intellect, in the same manner as Apollo is the solar intellect."[131] And with medicine is associated divination, the two being derivative from prudence: "She unfolds into light all the parts of divine and human prudence . . . the prophetic and the medicinal . . . the causes of these . . . antecedently comprehended in one divinity."[132] Perhaps to this conjunction of powers is to be ascribed the manner of her approach to the sick: "She [Isis] takes pleasure in curing men's bodies; and to those that desire her assistance, in their sleep she clearly manifests her presence, and affords ready and effectual relief to them that stand in need of it . . . for in sleep she is present with persons, and applies remedies to the sick, and wonderfully cures those that are her votaries. . . . They say she found out a medicine that would raise the dead to life, with which she not only raised her son Orus, that was killed by the Titans . . . but, by that application, made him immortal. . . ."[133] It is a passage to note, for it has an important bearing upon a point to be elaborated later in this discussion.

We read in Plutarch: "These are such as pretend, like the Greeks, that Saturn symbolizes *Time,* Juno the *Air,* the birth of Vulcan, the change of Air into *Fire;* and similarly amongst

[130] *Ibid.,* p. 2.
[131] *Proclus on the Timaeus,* Taylor, Vol. I, Bk. I, p. 134.
[132] *Ibid.,* p. 133.
[133] *Diodorus the Sicilian,* Booth, I, 31-32.

the Egyptians, that Osiris is the *Nile,* copulating with Isis the
Earth; Typhon, the *Sea,* into which the Nile flowing vanishes
and is dispersed. . . ."[134]   And again, the rationalization of
myth by Macrobius: "He goes on to interpret Jupiter not as
the highest God but as the heaven, and Juno as the air."[135]
The identification of the air is, however, more often with
Minerva as one of the triad constituting Juno.   Thus in
Diodorus Siculus: "To the air they gave the name Minerva,
signifying something proper to the nature thereof, and called
her the daughter of Jupiter, and counted a virgin, because the
air naturally is not subject to corruption, and is in the highest
part of the universe; whence rises the fable that she was the
issue of Jupiter's brain: they say she is called also Tritogeneia,
or thrice begotten, because she changes her natural qualities
thrice in the year, the spring, summer, and winter; and that
she was called Glaucopis, not that she hath grey eyes, (as some
of the Greeks have supposed, for that is a weak conceit) but
because the air seems to be of a gray colour, to the view."[136]

   The powers of the heavens are sometimes arranged in this
order, Sun, Moon, and Air, as being animated by three kinds
of fire: "Perhaps likewise the [Chaldaean] Oracles teach us
this, since they every where arrange the Moon after the Sun,
and the Air after the Moon, both when they deliver the order
of them from above, and when from beneath.   For they say,
'The aetherial course, the immense impulse of the Moon, and
the aerial streams.'   And again, 'O aether, Sun, spirit of the
Moon, and ye leaders of the air.' . . . Perhaps therefore, as I
have said, it is possible to be persuaded from the Oracles, that
the Sun is immediately prior to the Moon, as the Moon is
prior to the Air, all heaven having the order of fire. . . ."[137]

[134] *Plutarch's Morals,* King, p. 27.   [135] *Macrobius,* Whittaker, p. 69.
[136] *Diodorus the Sicilian,* Booth, I, 21.
[137] *Proclus on the Timaeus,* Taylor, Vol. II, Bk. IV, p. 225.

The close association of Moon and Air in the solar myth is explicable in the supposed influence of the Moon upon rainfall and dews. To the Egyptians, dependent for life upon the Nile, moisture is the creative principle and as such is worshipped in Isis, the Moon: ". . . The moist Principle being the Final Cause and origin of all things, has produced from the beginning the three first elements, Earth, Air, Fire. . . . For the Egyptians give the name of Jupiter to the *breath,* to which everything dry and fiery is antagonistic. This latter element is not the Sun, but has a certain affinity to the Sun; now moisture quenching the excess of dryness, augments and strengthens the exhalations by means of which the wind is nourished and made vigorous."[138]   And again, in Diodorus Siculus: "Isis likewise, being interpreted, signifies antient, that name being ascribed to the moon from eternal generations. . . . They say that these gods [Isis and Osiris] in their natures do contribute much to the generation of all things, the one being of a hot and active nature, the other moist and cold, but both having something of the air; and that by these, all things are both brought forth and nourished."[139]

The Egyptian priests, "remarking the Moon had an immediate influence on the atmosphere, wind, and rain, held her, as well as the Sun, to be the source of the inundation, and, seeking a characteristic epithet, named her Isis, which in Egyptian, signifies the cause of abundance."[140]   More especially is Isis associated in Egyptian mythology with the dews which preserve life in the periods of drought: "And whereas moisture generates creatures from heat, as from a seminal principle, things so generated, by being inwrapt in the dewy

---

[138] *Plutarch's Morals,* King, pp. 30-31.
[139] *Diodorus the Sicilian,* Booth, I, 19-20.
[140] Savary, *op. cit.,* II, p. 357.

mists of the night, grew and increased, and in the day solidated, and were made hard by the heat of the sun."[141]

The elaborations of the solar myth are explained by the rationalist as depicting the course of the seasons, the positions of sun and moon at various periods, the seasonal rainfall, the scorching winds, and drought: "Whoever has traveled, but a little, through this country, will observe physical phaenomena, concealed under the veil of fable. The wind Khamsin often is very destructive in spring, raising vortices of scorching sands which suffocate travelers, cloud the air, and hide the face of the sun, so that the earth, sometimes, remains plunged in darkness. Here are the death of Osiris, and the reign of Typhon. These tempests usually happen in the months of February, March, and April; but are dissipated when the sun approaches Leo, because it changes the atmosphere, and brings the Etesian winds which dispel unwholesome vapours, and maintain coolness, and salubrity, under a fiery sky. This is the triumph of Horus over Typhon, and this his glorious reign. Naturalists, observing the influence of the moon on the atmosphere, allied her to the god to chase the usurper from the throne."[142]

Plutarch rationalizes the sun myth in similar terms. Typhon means the drought which masters the Nile (Osiris). The Nile then recedes, the night lengthens, and darkness increases: "But when Isis has recovered Osiris, and is making Horus grow, strengthened by means of exhalations, clouds and mists, Typhon has been conquered indeed, but not destroyed, because the goddess of the Earth hath not suffered the Principle opposed to moisture to be entirely exterminated, but she lowered and slackened the same, wishing that the mixture might still continue: inasmuch as it was not possible

[141] *Diodorus the Sicilian*, Booth, I, 16.
[142] Savary, *op. cit.*, II, 340-41.

for the world to be complete if the fiery principle failed and
were exterminated, and if all this is not told in so many words,
yet one may not reasonably regret the story that Typhon of
old conquered the party of Osiris."[143]

Savary's rationalization of the ancient Egyptian myths is
full and of great interest, but as I have outlined it (Appendix
C) I shall only briefly stress some of its details. The Moon, Isis,
being the cause of abundance, is often also identified with the
earth, the mother of fruits.[144] Sometimes Isis is identified
only with "that part of Egypt which the Nile waters, alluding
to its fecundity."[145] In the dry season when Typhon pursues
the son of Osiris to destroy him "Isis confides him to Butis,
whose abode is amidst the waters. That is to say, the exhalations of the Sun and the influence of the Moon on the atmosphere, preventing those ills the Khamsin would cause, bestow the salutary dews which renovate nature. . . ."[146] These
dews depend upon the phases of the moon, the third phase,
from the 11th to the 15th being called "the perfect gift, because
the dews then fell abundantly."[147]

All manner of ceremonial and elaborate ritual grows up
about these seasonal phenomena in which the Moon ever
plays the chief rôle. She is a determining force in the lives
of mortals and in the generation of all animals and plants,
being the goddess of nature. In Plutarch we read: "So far,
then, is she separated from the sun by reason of her weight,
and approximated to earth, that if one must define substances by localities, the constitution and beauty of Earth attracts the moon, and she is of influence in matters and over
persons upon Earth, by reason of her relationship and
proximity."[148]

[143] *Plutarch's Morals*, King, p. 34.
[144] Savary, *op. cit.*, II, 361.
[145] *Ibid.*, p. 362.
[146] *Ibid.*, p. 380.
[147] *Ibid.*, p. 379.
[148] *Plutarch's Morals*, King, p. 210.

With this passage from Plutarch suggesting a gravitational pull upon the earth, or a magnetic attraction of earth and moon, a transition may be made to a body of scientific speculation dating from Gilbert and Newton in which are defined the forces of gravitation, electricity, and magnetism and the relationship of earth to moon as affected by them. I have elsewhere[149] shown that Newton and subsequent scientists to the time of Humphry Davy were seeking a basic principle or force to which all other forces might be reduced, and found in electricity the nearest approach, among physical phenomena, to the ether of Newton's hypothesis. Electricity, it was thought, might explain alike the attractions of the heavenly bodies, the nature of matter itself, and the spirit of animation. My immediate concern is to draw from so vast a body of speculation sufficient data to elucidate in the *Witch of Atlas* the manifest allusions to magnetism as a force closely related to, or identical with, electricity.

A few citations will make clear the early conception of the earth as a magnetic body generating streams of force which are magnetic or electric in character: "A magnetic body also may magnetize a number of non-magnetic bodies without losing any of its attractive powers, because of the awakening of potential magnetic tendencies in so-called non-magnetic bodies. Therefore we may say that all bodies are magnetic bodies whether their magnetic attraction be potential or actual. Newton, like Gilbert, thought also, as we have seen, that the 'force' of a body is the sum total of forces of each particle of which the body is composed. We must always keep in mind that Newton put in the same category all attracting forces, whether their function be gravity, magnetism, or electricity.

"Gilbert claimed that the earth is a great loadstone; it exhibits the same characteristics of attraction as any small or

[149] *A Newton Among Poets,* chaps. VI-VII.

great loadstone does. The interior of the earth, he thought, is composed of a homogeneous magnetic mass."[150]   And again: "From the above, as well as from some points to be stated later, Gilbert developed two general axioms or rules: (1) that 'the matter of the earth's globe is brought together and held together by itself electrically; (2) that the earth's globe is directed and revolves magnetically.' "[151]

We find in Boyle the belief "that there is always in the air a swarm of streams moving in a determinate course betwixt the north pole and the south";[152] Beccaria "conjectures that a regular and constant circulation of the whole mass of the electric fluid from north to south may be the original cause of *magnetism* in general."[153]   And again we read: "Kepler, Gassendus, Gilbert, and others, ascribe *gravity* to a certain magnetic attraction of the earth. These authors conceive the earth to be one great magnet continually emitting effluvia, which lay hold on all bodies, and draw them toward the earth."[154]

It is no concern of our argument to enter the scientific controversies of the eighteenth century and determine where the weight of authority lies. It suffices to demonstrate that there was justification for Shelley's belief that electricity and magnetism were identical or similar phenomena and that the earth's attraction was due to them. A passage from Beccaria will be of especial weight as it is evident that from Beccaria Shelley derived his knowledge of the part played by electricity

[150] Adolph Snow, *Matter and Gravity in Newton's Physical Philosophy*, pp. 176-77.

[151] *Ibid.*, pp. 177-78, Gilbert, *Loadstone and Magnetic Bodies* . . . , p. 97, quoted by Snow.

[152] *Ibid.*, p. 175, Boyle as quoted by Snow.

[153] Ephraim Chambers (ed.), *Cyclopedia; or, An Universal Dictionary of Arts and Sciences, sub* "Magnetism."

[154] *Ibid., sub* "Gravity."

in the atmosphere:[155] "Are not these peculiar effects of the
electric fire with respect to magnetism, so many proofs which
corroborate my former conjectures, that the peculiar magnetic
force observed in *load-stone,* is to be attributed to either atmospherical, or subterraneous, strokes of lightning; and that
the *universal systematical* properties of magnetic bodies, are
produced by an universal systematical circulation of the electric element?   It is true, magnetism is excited by other means
than electricity, such as heating, hammering, rubbing, break-
ing, etc., but is not common fire or heat, also excited in a
number of different ways; and yet it is always found to be
the principal agent, and, as it were, the author of its own
phenomena."[156]

Streams of electrical energy emanating from one of the
magnetic poles and entering the other, are in Beccaria's belief
the cause of the aurora borealis: "Signior Beccaria, who pursued his observations on atmospherical electricity farther than
any of his associates in these inquiries, conjectures that there
is a constant and regular circulation of the electric fluid from
north to south, which may be the original cause of magnetism in general; and he thinks, that the aurora borealis may
be this electric matter performing its circulation in such a
state of the atmosphere as renders it visible, or approaching
nearer the earth than usual."[157]

The earth, we have seen, may be thought of as a magnet
and the streams of force which it generates and which cir-
culate between the magnetic poles are electrical and magnetic
in character.   The force of attraction between the heavenly
bodies was also thought to be electric or magnetic in character.
It would follow that the attraction of earth to moon would

[155] See *A Newton Among Poets,* chap. VIII.

[156] Giovanni Beccaria, *A Treatise upon Artificial Electricity,* p. 310.

[157] Abraham Rees (ed.), *The Cyclopedia; or, Universal Dictionary of Arts,
Sciences, and Literature, sub* "Aurora Borealis."

set up streams of force between them. What use Shelley makes of this theme in *Prometheus* I have elsewhere demonstrated.[158] In the Promethean age, after the overthrow of Jupiter, the liberated force emanating from the earth is described as warming the frozen moon, thawing her seas, and restoring her atmosphere. The moon again becomes a habitable sphere.

If the earth and moon exert a magnetic attraction one upon the other, this attraction, as evidenced in the tides, varies with the phases of the moon, being strongest at the full and weakest in the dark of the moon. There are some speculations in Erasmus Darwin's *Zoonomia* from which I shall cite briefly, merely to show a possible suggestion for Shelley's practice in the *Witch*, though he need have had no scientific direction to an implication so clearly made: "On the side of the earth most distant from the moon, the moon's attraction is less, and the centrifugal force round their common center of motion is greater; both which contribute to raise the tides on that side of the earth. . . . On these accounts, when the moon is in the zenith or nadir, the gravitation of bodies on the earth's surface will be greatest at the two opposite quadratures. . . . Now when the sun and moon have their united gravitation on the same side of the earth, as at the new moon; or when the solar attraction coincides with the greater centrifugal motion of that side of the earth, which is furthest distant from the moon, as at the full moon; and when this happens about noon or midnight, the gravitation of terrene bodies towards the earth will be greater about six hours after noon, and after midnight, than at any other part of the lunar period. . . ."[159] From which technical discussion I wish to suggest no more than this, that the attraction of earth and

[158] *A Newton Among Poets*, pp. 155-64.
[159] II, 512-13.

moon, which we have already seen is magnetic, varies with the hour of day and night and with the phases of the moon.

The ancient scientists of the Nile valley, noting the relation of the moon to dewfall, attributed to her the highest powers as the preserver in resisting the assaults of Typhon, the evil principle personified in the hot blasting winds which suck up moisture and destroy vegetation. As Savary observes, the dews are heaviest in the full of the moon and are lightest in the dark of the moon. The electrical phenomena incident to dewfall are discussed by Beccaria in his interesting work upon atmospheric electricity, a work whose influence I believe to be apparent in *Prometheus*.[160] If the dews are accompanied by electric action, and if the moon in her phases determines the dewfall, the relationship of the moon to the electric phenomena of the atmosphere is evident. The whole of Shelley's natural history insofar as it relates to the earth and moon implies some interplay of force between the two—gravitational, electric, magnetic—this varying as the moon draws nearer or recedes in her erratic course. It is important, therefore, to dwell for a moment upon the electrical phenomena of the dew as one evidence of the influence of the moon upon the earth's atmosphere.

"The electricity of dew," says Beccaria, "depends, it seems, on the quantity of the dew, as the electricity of rain depends on the quantity of rain; and the peculiar manner after which this dew takes place, influences the electricity, in the same way as does the peculiar manner in which the rain likewise takes place."[161] Beccaria notes, also, that "the electricity of dew seems to have, as it were, an inclination to appear for several evenings successively, with the same characters."[162] The trend of Beccaria's observations is that in serene weather the atmos-

---

[160] *A Newton Among Poets,* chap. VIII.
[161] Beccaria, *op. cit.,* p. 468.   [162] *Ibid.*

phere empties itself of electricity at nighttime by means of
the dewfall and renews itself at sunrise when the water vapor
is drawn again into the atmosphere. Electricity is attendant
upon moisture, and the moon, be it remembered, is traditionally the goddess of moisture, creating mists and vapours, and
the dew. "If to all the above observations, we add the consideration of the peculiar electricity of *dew,* with which I pro-
pose to conclude, and that of winds, which, in proportion to
their dampness, as I shall presently relate, increase the fre-
quency of the electricity of clear weather, we shall certainly
find it as evident a truth as any in Natural Philosophy, that
the moisture in the air is the conductor of this electricity."[163]
Clearly, had the ancients known the activities of atmospheric
electricity, Isis, the moon goddess, would have been the presiding deity of this, as of moisture and the dew.

This has been a long parenthesis in our argument upon the
Witch of Atlas, but it has served to intimate the vast background of physical and metaphysical lore relating to the moon
and will make possible a more rapid progress henceforth. To
return, then, to stanza XLVII with its employment of lunar
phenomena—

> Or when the weary moon was in the wane,
> Or in the noon of interlunar night,
> The Lady-Witch in visions could not chain
> Her spirit; but sailed forth under the light
> Of shooting stars, and bade extend amain
> Its storm-outspeeding wings the Hermaphrodite;
> She to the Austral waters took her way,
> Beyond the fabulous Thamondocana.

In the dark of the moon the Witch speeds on the lightning to
the southern hemisphere, beyond Thamondocana, which is
Timbuktoo.

I need hardly stress the electrical phenomena of this pas-

[163] *Ibid.,* pp. 459-60.

sage in the allusions to the shooting stars and the Hermaphrodite. More obscure is the Witch's flight to the Southern hemisphere, though there are passages explanatory of the solar myth which suggest a partial meaning. Thus we read in Savary: "Philosophers . . . by Night, Athor, and Venus, meant that season when the sun, having passed the equator, remains in the austral hemisphere; the days then being shorter and the nights longer."[164] Savary cites Macrobius to the effect that Venus, the upper hemisphere, weeps the passage of the sun into the austral hemisphere, which is the realm of Proserpine, who there detains the sun during the winter season.[165] Again we read that the waning of the moon is caused by the evil Typhon, who creates storms and whirlwinds: "Hence this principle [Typhon] is weak and inoperative here below, mingling itself and clinging close to such members as are subject to corruption and to change, it is the creator of earthquakes and tremors in the ground, of droughts in the air, and strange blasts; and, again, of whirlwinds and lightnings, and it infects waters and winds with pestilences, and rears up and tosses itself as far as the Moon, oftentimes checking and darkening her lustre, as the Egyptians believe. And they tell that Typhon at one time hit Horus; at another struck out his eye and swallowed it up, and then gave it back to the Sun; signifying by *blow* the monthly waning of the Moon, by *blinding,* her eclipse, which the Sun remedies, when he again reflects himself upon her, after she has passed through the shadow of the earth."[166]

The succeeding stanzas, XLVIII to L, are pertinent to the description of stormy Typhon and his conquest, whether in the winter or in the dark of the moon, of the good principle in nature symbolized by the moon. For the Witch, by her

---

[164] Savary, *op. cit.,* II, 307.
[165] *Ibid.*   [166] *Plutarch's Morals,* King, p. 48.

Austral lake builds herself "a windless haven" where she is safe from the storms which rage around her. A reading of these stanzas in terms of the sun-myth is easy, but if, as we have seen thus far to be the case, the Witch symbolizes also electric and magnetic energy, her retreat to the southern hemisphere should be intelligible also in these terms.

If, as we have already inferred, Shelley is rationalizing the sun myth in terms of a modern meteorology, the retreat of the sun in winter would imply a diminution of solar and electric energy in the northern hemisphere; and the waning of the moon likewise would be manifest in a diminution of magnetic energy as created by the attraction of earth and moon. Terrestrial energy, as expressed in electricity and magnetism, would then at these times be concentrated in the southern hemisphere. I believe, therefore, that the austral lake symbolizes a fountain of energy to which the Witch retreats in times of storm and cold and that this may be thought of as the south magnetic pole,[167] whose location would be, geographically, "beyond the fabulous Thamondocana," or Timbuktoo. The suggestion anticipates a more convincing proof that the Witch is to be identified with magnetism and I shall recall it again in its proper time.

The phenomena of the next half dozen stanzas are, whatever may be our provisional reservations as to the identification of the magnetic pole, all electrical in character. The Witch builds herself a "windless haven out of the clouds," an activity of the atmospheric electricity, for "This accumulation of electric matter also evidently contributes to support the atmospheric vapor when it is condensed into the form of clouds."[168]

---

[167] See Paul Mottclay, *Bibliographical History of Electricity and Magnetism* for Halley's theory (1683) of magnetic poles near poles of earth. By poles he meant places where the magnetic force was at a maximum.
[168] Darwin, *Botanic Garden*, I, 63, note.

The austral lake, walled thus from storms, is a place of calm where the Lady plays her pranks upon the water, in her light boat "circling the image of a shooting star" until "the car of the late moon" began "to journey from the misty east."

Thereupon a host of atmospheric phenomena are recorded. Her "ministering spirits" are summoned from the high clouds, the legions with their "meteor flags" who build a "proud pavilion of the intertexture of the atmosphere." This "imperial tent" is made of "woven exhalations underlaid with lambent lightning-fire" and there is also "a tapestry of fleece-like mist." Her throne is set upon "those wandering isles of aëry dew which highest shoals of mountain shipwreck not"—the clouds of water vapor existing in the highest atmosphere. It is a passage which in its general electric implication is self evident. I shall cite but one quotation in its support: "All the vapors, or moist effluvia whatever, which are anyhow brought to rise in the atmosphere, or which swim, or descend in it, are affected by the aërial electricity. . . ."[169]

Of the nature of her ministers, the aerial electricity in its various manifestations, there can be no doubt, but the lines which report their intelligence of the happenings between earth and moon evidently assume their magnetic no less than their electric character and their dependence upon the moon. For they are depicted as bringing intelligence to the Witch, after an interval which corresponds with the dark of the moon, of all the happenings in the interlunar sphere. In the dark of the moon, it is evident, they are not active and the occurrences of the "celestial earth" are unknown.

There is to this passage an unmistakable neo-Platonic flavor, for the moon and the region between earth and moon are the home of the genii and daemons who are the agents of the gods: "The genii do not always pass their time upon

[169] Beccaria, *op. cit.,* p. 445.

her (the moon), but they come down hither and take charge
of Oracles; they are present at and assist in the most advanced
of the initiatory rites [in the several Mysteries], as punishers
and keepers of wrongdoers they act, and shine as saviours in
battle and at sea. . . ."[170] We read also in Cudworth, paraphrasing Varro, "That from the highest circuit of the heavens
to the sphere of the moon there are ethereal souls or animals,
the stars which are not only understood, but also seen to be
celestial gods; and between the sphere of the moon and the
middle region of the air, there are aereal souls or animals,
which though not seen by our eyes, yet are discovered by our
mind, and called heroes, lares, and genii."[171] It is from these
daemons and genii, apparently, that the aerial agents of the
Witch, electric and magnetic, bring the news of the happenings beneath the moon; either that or the aerial forces are
themselves to be identified as these daemons and genii. In
either case the scientific and neo-Platonic mythologies, here as
elsewhere, are poetically blent.

The activities of the Witch described in stanzas LV and
LVI are all such as pertain to the phenomena of atmospheric
electricity. She rides the clouds and follows the lightning's
track. And sometimes she ascends "to those streams of upper
air, which whirl the earth in its diurnal round." This "upper
air" is presumably the atmosphere of hydrogen which Darwin
supposes to surround the rare air, a region of various electric
phenomena and the origin of fireballs and the aurora borealis;[172] these phenomena are caused by the fusion of hydrogen
and common air by means of atmospheric electricity. The
electric streams emanate from and return to the earth. When
visibly manifest they are thus described in *Prometheus*:

[170] *Plutarch's Morals,* King, pp. 254-55.
[171] Cudworth, *op. cit.,* II, 367.
[172] *Botanic Garden,* I, Additional Note No. I.

Vast beams like spokes from some invisible wheel
Which whirl as the orb whirls, swifter than thought,
Filling the abyss with sun-like lightenings.[173]
                                        —*P. U.* IV, ll. 274-76.

Therein the streams of energy circulating between the poles
are made visible as the aurora borealis. These are within
the "streams of upper air which whirl the earth in its diurnal
round." Darwin ascribes to the stratosphere of hydrogen the
origin of the luminous manifestation of electric phenomena in
the upper air.

On those days in which the Witch ascends to the "streams
of upper air" mortals find the sky "calm and fair." Here
again the allusion is obviously to atmospheric electricity. I
have discussed this point, an important one, in *Prometheus,*
with citations from Beccaria's work on the activities of atmospheric electricity in serene weather.[174] It was his observation
that the intensity of atmospheric electricity was greatest in
sunny days undisturbed by wind. For the immediate proof
of this general meteorological background I deem one sentence from Beccaria will here suffice: "Impetuous winds use
to lessen the intensity of the electricity of clear weather."[175]

In the ensuing stanzas the activities of the Witch are mostly
mental rather than physical and the lore which explains these
is in part neo-Platonic, for *"the Nile also is a symbol of the
life which is poured on the whole world."*[176] Apis, Serapis,
avatars of Osiris, are associated with the Nile, but more especially is Isis the genius of that stream and so, in the neo-
Platonic interpretation, the goddess of production. In the rationalization of the sun myth we read: "The Nile began to
increase at the new Moon after the solstice, wherefore, the

---

[173] See *A Newton Among Poets,* pp. 172-74.
[174] *A Newton Among Poets,* pp. 120-21.
[175] *Op. cit.,* p. 460.
[176] *Proclus on the Timaeus,* Taylor, Vol. I, Bk. I, p. 81.

priests, holding this planet to be the mother of the winds, de-
creed her the honour. 'Isis is the genius of the Nile. The
sistrum she holds in her right hand signified the increase and
flooding of the waters, the vase in her left their abundance
in the canals. . . .' According to Pausanias, the Egyptians
were persuaded the tears of Isis augmented the Nile, and made
it overflow the fields, of which superstition the Copts are not
yet cured; they still say a dew falls at the solstice, which fer-
ments the water of the river, and produces the flood. . . .
'They say the degrees of the elevation of the waters answer to
the phases of the Moon.' "[177]

Water in the ancient philosophy is the symbol of matter,
and a stream the symbol of existence flowing to its reunion
with the sea. So great, however, is the Nile that it is, in
Egyptian theology, often identified with the sea: "But the
Egyptians account their Nile to be Oceanus, at which all the
gods were born."[178] The Witch in her journeys down the
Nile, it will be noted, passes not only on the surface, observing
the stream's progress through places famed in ancient lore, but
also "under the Nile" and in "calm depths." She does so in
her dual rôle as Minerva, to whom certain Egyptian cities are
sacred, and as the goddess of love and intellectual beauty
animating the deeps of life. Of Minerva we learn that in
Egypt she "is allotted the city which is named after her, and
also . . . Saïs."[179] The spiritual activities of the goddess below "the liquid surface of man's life" are more complex and
cast new light upon the poet's conception of her character and
powers.

It should first be noted in these stanzas that the general
figure is one familiar in Shelley's frequent use of it, the figure

[177] Savary, *op. cit.*, II, pp. 359-60.
[178] *Diodorus the Sicilian*, Booth, I, 20-21.
[179] *Proclus on the Timaeus*, Taylor, Vol. I, Bk. I, p. 118.

which likens all life to a sea, symbol of unity, whose surface is broken into waves, symbol of the individual life. I have earlier referred to the employment of this figure in Asia's journey on the stream of preëxistence wherein she speaks of

> Manhood's dark and tossing waves
> —*P. U.* II, 5, l. 99.

and wherein the sea is the symbol of unity and the reunion of the soul with the infinite. More notable still is the passage:

> We come from the mind
> Of humankind,
> Which was late so dusk, and obscene, and blind;
> Now 't is an ocean
> Of clear emotion,
> A heaven of serene and mighty motion.
>
> From that deep abyss
> Of wonder and bliss,
> Whose caverns are crystal palaces. . . .
> —*P. U.,* IV, ll. 93-101.

The figure here employs the ocean as the symbol of the unity of all human mind, and the crystal caverns as the symbol of the individual mind, translucent as implying its unity with other mind yet also separate; a symbol analogous to that of the waves of the sea which are a part of the one ocean of being and yet separate and distinct. Both images are instances of Shelley's attempt to depict multiplicity in unity.

In stanza LXIII of the *Witch* a variant of the same figure is employed:

> We, the weak mariners of that wide lake,
> Where'er its shores extend or billows roll,
> Our course unpiloted and starless make
> O'er its wild surface to an unknown goal;
> But she in the calm depths her way could take,
> Where in bright bowers immortal forms abide,
> Beneath the weltering of the restless tide.

The thought is the familiar neo-Platonic one of the unreality of earthly existence. True existence lies in the realm of intellectual being, of which each earthly soul partakes and to which it ultimately returns. The Witch pursues her way through the unity of being in which the slumbering soul reveals its true nature, its "immortal form" slumbering now during its earthly incarnation.

The Witch wandering among the sleeping souls of mortals scatters "sweet visions from her presence sweet." Minerva, we have previously seen, is the goddess of medicine and, appearing in dreams, aids the patient to the diagnosis of his own illness and cure. But the visions of sleep are sometimes more than this. In them the soul may perceive glimpses of reality such as it was the purpose of the Eleusinian Mysteries to evoke, in which "divine *initiation,* we became *spectators* of entire, simple, immovable and *blessed visions,* resident in a pure light; and were ourselves pure and immaculate, being liberated from this surrounding vestment, which we denominate body."[180]   It is such "sweet visions" apparently that the presence of the Witch inspires.

The sleep in which lie these mortal forms is the sleep of mortality through which the Lady perceives their true natures. Shelley's familiar

> Death is the veil which those who live call life;
> They sleep and it is lifted;
> —*P. U.* III, 3, ll. 113-114.

has many parallels in the ancient philosophies and in neo-Platonism. We read in Heraclitus that "Death is what we see waking. What we see in sleep is a dream."[181]   In Taylor: "These wise men universally considered Hell or death as com-

[180] Taylor, *Eleusinian and Bacchic Mysteries,* p. 103.
[181] *The Fragments of the Work of Heraclitus of Ephesus on Nature* (trans. by G. T. W. Patrick), p. 100.

mencing in the present life (as we have abundantly proved),
and that, consequently, sense is nothing more than the energy
of the dormant soul, and a perception, as it were, of the delusions of dreams."[182]   And again: "The soul's punishment
and existence hereafter are nothing more than a continuation
of its state at present, and a transmigration, as it were, from
sleep to sleep, and from dream to dream."[183]   The instances
are numerous.   Two more must suffice: *"Whatever we see*
when awake, is death; and when asleep a dream."[184]   And
last, Plutarch quoting Heraclitus: "To those who are awake,
there is one world in common, but of those who are asleep,
each is withdrawn to a private world of his own."[185]

What then of the "charm of strange device" which the
Witch employs and

> . . . murmured on mute lips with tender tone,
> Could make that spirit mingle with her own.
> *W. of A.* ll. 575-76.

We read that

> To those she saw most beautiful, she gave
> Strange panacea in a crystal bowl;
> They drank in their deep sleep of that sweet wave,
> And lived thenceforward as if some control,
> Mightier than life, were in them. . . .
> —*W. of A.* ll. 593-97.

Previously, in stanza XVII, we have encountered a similar
passage.   There we read of

> . . . liquors clear and sweet, whose healthful might
> Could medicine the sick soul to happy sleep,
> And change eternal death into a night
> Of glorious dreams—or, if eyes needs must weep,
> Could make their tears all wonder and delight—
> She in her crystal vials did closely keep.
> —*W. of A.* ll. 177-82.

[182] Taylor, *Eleusinian and Bacchic Mysteries,* pp. 80-81.
[183] *Ibid.,* p. 36.   [184] *Ibid.,* p. 38.
[185] *Heraclitus on Nature,* Patrick, p. 107.

The "crystal bowl" and the "crystal vials" are employed to the same end, to induce sweet dreams to the sick soul. Is there a more specific meaning from these lines than that the Witch, Minerva, goddess of medicine and appearing in dreams, comforts the sick?

Let me recall some of the magic treasures of the Witch as recorded in stanzas XIV-XVII:

> . . . sounds of air
> Which had the power all spirits of compelling,
> Folded in cells of crystal silence. . . .

and

> . . . Visions swift, and sweet, and quaint,
> Each in its thin sheaf, like a chrysalis

and

> . . . odors in a kind of aviary
> To stir sweet thoughts or sad, in destined minds

and, last, the "liquors clear and sweet" in their "crystal vials." These are some of the treasures of the Witch who "scatters sweet visions" and offers a "strange panacea in a crystal bowl" and possesses a "charm of strange device" which "murmured on mute lips" can make "that spirit mingle with her own." Thus grouped, these powers, and the way of the Witch in their employment, are highly suggestive, but before guessing their meaning let me cite a passage from another poem of Shelley's.

These are three stanzas pertinent to our solution of the meaning of the Witch in her rôle as healer and of her "charm of strange device":

> Sleep, sleep on! forget thy pain;
> My hand is on thy brow,
> My spirit on thy brain;
> My pity on thy heart, poor friend;
> And from my fingers flow

The powers of life, and like a sign,
Seal thee from thine hour of woe;
And brood on thee, but may not blend
With thine.

. . . .

Sleep, sleep, and with the slumber of
The dead and the unborn
Forget thy life and love;
Forget that thou must wake forever;
Forget the world's dull scorn;
Forget lost health, and the divine
Feelings which died in youth's brief morn;
And forget me, for I can never
Be thine.

Like a cloud big with a May shower,
My soul weeps healing rain
On thee, thou withered flower;
It breathes mute music on thy sleep;
Its odour calms thy brain!
Its light within thy gloomy breast
Spreads like a second youth again.
By mine thy being is to its deep
Possest.

These are lines entitled "The Magnetic Lady to her Patient"
and were written "For Jane and Williams only to see."

What we know of Shelley's experiments with animal magnetism or mesmerism we learn from Medwin's account in the
Shelley Papers: "I had seen magnetism practised in India and
at Paris, and at his earnest request consented to try its efficacy.
Mesmer himself could not have hoped for more complete suc-
cess. The imposition of my hand on his forehead instantaneously put a stop to the spasm, and threw him into a
magnetic sleep, which for want of a better word is called
somnambulism." To questions put to Shelley while in trance
asking the nature of his complaint he replied in Italian, "What
would cure me would kill me." It is evident that Shelley
had a first hand acquaintance with the "magnetic sleep" and

his description of it is presumably exact. The correspondences in his description with the passages enumerated in the *Witch,* therefore, take on more than a casual significance. The lines

> Sleep, sleep, and with the slumber of
> The dead and the unborn

and

> My soul weeps healing rain,
>   On thee, thou withered flower;
> It breathes mute music on thy sleep;
>   Its odour calms thy brain!
> Its light within thy gloomy breast
> Spreads like a second youth again

have an evident correspondence with the endowments of the Witch and with the practice of her healing power which we have not as yet considered.

Before examining in detail the Witch's exercise of her power, the "strange panacea" which she gives, I wish to remark on several contributory points which make the identification of the Witch's healing power with "animal magnetism" or hypnotism more conclusive. Shelley's own experience of the magnetic trance is, of course, the most compelling evidence, but his and Medwin's interest in this therapeutic agency reveals their knowledge of Mesmer's practices in magnetic healing. These, which excited so widespread an interest that Mesmer was finally examined by a commission of doctors and his achievements falsely discredited, were but a part of that experiment and speculation which exercised the natural philosophers at the end of the eighteenth century, a speculation which sought to identify electricity and magnetism with the spirit of animation. I have elsewhere[186] cited sufficient evidence in proof of my contention and shall not here repeat it. A quotation from Mesmer will, however, per-

---

[186] *A Newton Among Poets,* pp. 57, 94-97.

tinently illustrate this latter search for a philosopher's stone, a universal principle in nature. Mesmer remarks in his memoir upon the discovery of animal magnetism that he was led to the "conviction that there does exist in nature a universal principle, which, independently of ourselves, performs all that we vaguely attribute to nature or to art."[187]

There is an interesting connection of this modern speculation as to the curative powers of magnetism with the ancient mythology and its rationalization. Minerva, goddess of medicine, supposedly, as the result of prayer, appeared to the sick man in his sleep and prompted him to the diagnosis of his own ailment. The similarity of this to the suggestion of the magnetic trance and to Shelley's recorded experience are evident. Moreover in the hospitals or sanitoria attached to the famous healing shrines of the ancient world where this therapy was practiced under the supervision of the priests there is no doubt in my mind that a form of hynotism was employed. Certainly the correspondences of Mesmer's practices with the legendary practices of the ancients is striking enough and leads to the inference I have made.

Curious as may seem this ascription to the Witch of healing powers identifiable with animal magnetism, there is much in the writings of Mesmer to corroborate the hypothesis. Especially pertinent is his thesis that the planets exert an influence upon the human body analogous to the influence of the sun and moon upon the sea. As there are tides due to the attraction of these heavenly bodies, so too there is an ebb and flow in human bodies of a subtle fluid emanating from the planets and akin to terrestrial magnetism. This he thinks the most tenuous of fluids, occupying all the pores of matter. He thinks of it seemingly as something like electricity[188] for he

---

[187] Mottelay, *op. cit.*, entry for 1772.

[188] F. A. Mesmer, *Memoires et Aphorismes de* . . . , par J. J. A. Ricard, p. 75.

speaks of it in one place as an invisible fire: "Le magnétisme animal, considéré comme un agent, est donc effectivement un feu invisible; il s'agit." But it will be well to quote at length the passage in which Mesmer ascribes the ebb and flow of animal magnetism to the operation of the planets in the same way that the force of gravitation causes the tides in the sea and air.

D'après mes idées sur cette matière, je donnai à Vienne, en 1766, une dissertation *De l'influence des planètes sur le corps humain.* J'avançais, d'après les principes connus de l'attraction universelle, constatée par les observations qui nous apprennent que les planètes s'affectent mutuellement dans leurs orbites, et que la lune et le soleil causent et dirigent sur notre globe le flux et le reflux dans la mer, ainsi que dans l'atmosphère; j'avançais, dis-je, que ces sphères exercent aussi une action directe sur toutes les parties constitutives des corps animés, particulièrement sur le *système nerveux,* moyennant un fluide qui pénètre tout: je déterminais cette action par L'INTENSION ET LA REMISSION des propriétés de la *matière et des corps organisés,* telles que sont la *gravité,* la *cohésion, l'élasticité, l'irritabilité, l'électricité.*

Je soutenais que, de même que les effets alternatifs, à l'égard de la gravité, produisent dans la mer le phénomène sensible que nous appelons flux et reflux, L'INTENSION ET LA REMISSION desdites propriétés, étant sujettes à l'action du même principe, occasionnent, dans les corps animés, des effets alternatifs analogues à ceux qu'éprouve la mer. Par ces considérations, j'établissais que le corps animal, étant soumis à la même action, éprouvait aussi une sorte de *flux* et *reflux.* J'appuyais cette théorie de différents exemples de révolutions périodiques. Je nommais la propriété du corps animal qui le rend susceptible de l'action des corps célestes et de la terre MAGNETISME ANIMAL; j'expliquais par ce magnétisme les révolutions périodiques que nous remarquons dans le sexe, et généralement celles que les médecins de tous les temps et de tous les pays ont observées dans les maladies.[189]

Mesmer contends that this animal magnetism is not, however, the same as mineral magnetism nor is it dependent upon electricity, though seemingly he regards it as akin to these

[189] *Ibid.,* pp. 8-9.

and its operation in the cure of disease facilitated by them. "Cette Académie n'a pas seule donné dans l'erreur de confondre le MAGNÉTISME ANIMAL avec le minéral, quoique j'aie toujours persisté dan mes écrits à établir que l'usage de l'aimant, quoique utile, était toujours imparfait sans le secours de la théorie du magnétisme animal."[190] Other critics, because he employs also electricity in his therapy, ascribe his cures to that. Therefore, he declares, "Le désir d'écarter pour jamais de semblables erreurs, et de mettre la verité dans son jour, m'a déterminé à ne plus faire aucun usage de l'électricité ni de l'aimant depuis 1779."[191] And again he elsewhere remarks "qu'on ne doit pas confondre le magnétisme avec les phénomènes qui ont pu donner lieu à ce qu'on veut appeler *l'électricité animale*."[192] But though animal magnetism is not the same as the magnetism evident in minerals, it seems to depend on the magnetic currents of the earth, for he remarks that there are two universal currents relative to man: "la gravité, et le courant magnétique d'un pôle à l'autre."[193]

It is Mesmer's belief that "nous sommes doués d'un sens *intérieur* qui est en relation avec l'ensemble de l'univers, et qui pourrait être considéré comme une *extension* de la vue."[194] This sense can, "dans cet état de crise,"[195] foresee events and recall the most distant past; it can project itself to any distance and in any direction.[196] Moreover, "le phénomène le plus commun est de voir l'intérieur de leur corps, et même celui des autres, et de juger avec la plus grande exactitude les maladies, leur marche, les remèdes nécessaires et leur effets."[197] This last citation is most interesting as linking up Mesmer's practices with those in the ancient temples of healing wherein the goddess Minerva was wont to appear in

[190] *Ibid.*, p. 23.
[191] *Ibid.*, p. 24.
[192] *Ibid.*, p. 77.
[193] *Ibid.*, p. 125.
[194] *Ibid.*, p. 79.
[195] *Ibid.*, p. 80.
[196] *Ibid.*, p. 81.
[197] *Ibid.*

dreams to the sick and tell them the nature and the curative means of their maladies. It is evident that the phenomena in the two instances, however designated and explained, are the same.

I have supposed these phenomena to be those of the hypnotic trance but it is not clear to me, if so, that Mesmer himself understood how he effected his cures. He gives elaborate directions as to the proper placing of the patient's body, the laying on of hands, and the effective employment of various apparatus involving chiefly magnetised water in tubs and bottles. . . . "On y place quatre ou un plus grand nombre de bouteilles à volonté, préparées et rangées comme celles du baquet."[198] And again, "l'intervalle des bouteilles se remplit de verre pilé ou sec ou humecté; une corde entortillée autour du goulot de chaque bouteille les fait communiquer ensemble"[199] etc. We learn also how the bottle may be magnetized:

Pour magnétiser une bouteille, vous la prenez par les deux extrémités, que vous frottez avec les doigts, en ramenant le mouvement au bord. Vous écartez la main successivement de ces deux extrémités en comprimant, pour ainsi dire, le fluide; vous prenez un verre ou un vase quelconque de la même manière, et vous magnétisez ainsi le fluide qu'il contient, en observant de le présenter à celui qui doit le boire, en le tenant entre le pouce et le petit doigt, et faisant boire dans cette direction: le malade y trouve un goût qui n'existerait pas, s'il buvait dans le sens opposé.[200]

This would seem to the unprofessional mind largely inadvertent quackery and irrelevant to the true agent employed. One or two passages support this view. In one place Mesmer remarks that a patient susceptible to the crisis, which I suppose to be the trance state, will often fall into it if, when he has been magnetized after the usual fashion, he is made to fix his eyes for some minutes upon the hand of a watch.[201]

[198] *Ibid.*, p. 161.
[199] *Ibid.*, pp. 161-162.
[200] *Ibid.*, p. 165.
[201] *Ibid.*, p. 187.

And in another place he tells how the patient may be magnetized by means of mirrors which reflect the magnetic rays upon the affected part.[202] In these instances one suspects the inducement of trance by means of a fixed attention upon a bright object. Likewise the crisis is induced by the piano and other instruments whose tones are conductors of the magnetic fluid and "de l'électricité naturelle des vaisseaux de cristal qui les produit."[203]

I had at first surmised the crystal vials wherewith the Witch dispenses her blissful dreams to be the crystal spheres employed in self-hypnosis. But this is, admittedly, but a guess. It may be, in the light of these excerpts from Mesmer, that the crystal vials are no more than the bottles with their magnetic waters supposedly inducing the healing trance. Or again Shelley may mean, as in the last citation, the crystal vessel of the electric machine in which, by friction, an electric charge is produced. I have no means of knowing how greatly he subscribed to Mesmer's theories, but inasmuch as these in some respects coincide with Shelley's evident scientific philosophy and inasmuch as Shelley himself had experienced, and beneficially, magnetic healing, they must be allowed considerable weight. Mesmer's universal element emanating from the planets and penetrating all matter is kindred to the ether of Newton's theory and to electricity, to which, in the advanced speculation of Shelley's time, various forms of energy were ascribed as derivative. Mesmer's speculation is in line with the effort of the age to find a unifying force, a single creative agent responsible both for matter and for the animating principle. That this scientific theory is also in accord with neo-Platonic speculation as to the nature of the universe is evident.

For the interpretation of the *Witch of Atlas* I should, how-

[202] *Ibid.*, pp. 196-97.   [203] *Ibid.*, pp. 197-98.

ever, attach most importance to Mesmer's belief that the mysterious animal magnetism ebbs and flows in harmony with the heavenly bodies.   This theory links perfectly with the ascription to Minerva, goddess of the upper air, of electric and magnetic forces which vary with the phases of the moon.   One brief concluding citation from Mesmer stresses this ebb and flow of the planetary forces, especially the varying influence of the moon upon terrestrial things, not only the air and the sea, but the mysterious vital currents in living creatures.

Il est donc une loi constante dans la nature, c'est qu'il y a une influence mutuelle sur la totalité de ces corps, et conséquemment elle s'exerce sur toutes les parties constitutives et sur leurs propriétés.

Cette influence réciproque et les rapports de tous les corps coexistants forment ce qu'on appelle *magnétisme*.[204]

.   .   .   .

Cette action à l'égard de la position respective de la terre et de la lune est plus forte dans les équinoxes.

1. Puisque la tendance centrifuge sous l'équateur est plus considérable, la gravité des eaux et de l'atmosphère y est plus faible.

2. Puisque l'action du soleil concourt avec celle de la lune, cette action est encore plus forte lorsque la lune est dans les signes boréaux, lorsqu'elle est en opposition ou en conjonction avec le soleil.[205]

Let me consider stanzas LXIX to LXXV in the light of our hypothesis and see whether the phenomena described are in accord with those of the "magnetic sleep."   Those who "in their deep sleep" drink the "strange panacea in a crystal bowl" it is said "live thenceforward as if some control mightier than life were in them."   This description fits completely the control exercised by the hypnotist over his patient.   What then of the lines which follow?

> . . . and the grave
> Of such, when death oppressed the weary soul,
> Was as a green and over-arching bower
> Lit by the gems of many a starry flower.
>
> —*W. of A.* ll. 597-600.

[204] *Ibid.*, p. 115.   [205] *Ibid.*, pp. 122-23.

Shelley's conception here apparently runs beyond the demonstrable practices of magnetic healing into the realm of neo-Platonism which held, as I have shown by previous citation, that life is but a dream and that the soul's existence hereafter is but a "transmigration, as it were, from sleep to sleep, and from dream to dream," and again that "whatever we see awake is death; and when asleep a dream." Shelley's thought seems to be that the Witch, who has power to give her "strange panacea" in life, has power also over those who lie in the trance or sleep of death. Both earthly life and death are, in the neo-Platonic philosophy, unreal in the sense that the soul is not therein yet freed from mortality. Only as it escapes from the flesh and the heritage of the flesh in the continuing life of the soul is it free to resume its heavenly existence in the realm of the mind, which is the place of true awakening, of life and reality. The Witch seemingly has power to comfort the soul in its transitional phase and endue its dreams with beauty.

Death, then, is no more a reality than earthly life, and the Witch makes "a mimic day within that deathly nook," the grave. Therein the body lies "age after age"; it is

> Mute, breathing, beating, warm, and undecaying,
> Like one asleep in a green hermitage.
> —*W. of A.* ll. 610-11.

In its dreams it is "beyond the rage of death or life." The conception is in accord with the teachings of neo-Platonism, however mystical and obscure these may seem. The power which can bring happiness in the dream of life "to those she saw most beautiful" can bring happiness also to those in the dream of death, for heaven and hell exist in the soul, whether in this life or in death, until it is released from the heritage of mortality and returns to the One.

Upon the brains "of those who were less beautiful" the

Witch "would write strange dreams." In these, men of evil mind are shown the futility of their purposes. The miser, the "lying scribe," the priest who deceives the credulous, king and courtier and soldier are shown the vanity of their pursuits. In these dreams the priests confess their deceptions and bid the herald "stick the same against the temple doors"; the king dresses an ape in the kingly crown and robes; the soldiers beat their swords to ploughshares; and the gaolers free "those of the liberal schism." These confessional dreams are consonant with the revelations ascribed to the patient when under control of the hypnotist.

There is in this connection an interesting link between the spiritual magnetic powers of the Witch and the physical magnetism which I have associated with the fiery lake or fountain in which she takes refuge from the wintry storms. In seeking for a suggestion in the older literature which might have prompted Shelley to his description, I chanced upon the following passage in Diodorus Siculus: "For they say, there [Ethiopia] is a four-square lake, an hundred and sixty feet in circuit, the water of which is in colour like unto vermilion, and of an extraordinary sweet flavour, much like unto old wine; yet of such wonderful operation, that whosoever drinks of it goes presently mad, and confesses all the faults that ever he had been before guilty of; but some will scarce believe this relation."[206] The correspondences here are curious. The "sweet wave" of which the beautiful souls drink is analogous to the "sweet flavour, much like unto old wine" of the lake. The waters of the lake drive those who drink to confession of their faults, as do the dreams which the Witch sends to the "less beautiful" souls. The red lake, moreover, is like the "well of crimson fire" to which the Lady resorts in the time of the wintry storms and which, as I have endeavored to show,

[206] *Diodorus the Sicilian,* Booth, I, 111.

may plausibly be a fount of energy at the south magnetic pole. In the endeavor to track the processes of the creative mind, this possible linking of the physical and mental forces of magnetism by means of the vermilion lake is not to be ignored. It is a point neither to be proved nor disproved. It is but one additional hint consonant with the interpretation of the *Witch* which, with so tedious a weight of citation and authority, I have endeavored to establish.

There remains one more difficult passage to interpret, the stanzas concerning the lovers whose intercourse which they think "only in fancy" proves, when "the tenth moon shone," to have been in actuality. It might simply be said of this that the lovers, in some wise entranced, were prompted to deeds of which later they were unsure. Yet in its context this passage, which follows the confessional revelations of dream wherein priest and king and soldier are made to show their true natures, seems rather to imply that what is intensely imagined takes on actuality in the world of sense and matter. If Shelley means this it is a curious and mystical idea but one which has parallels in neo-Platonic and theosophical literature. I shall cite a few passages in evidence.

In Proclus we read "That the demiurgic intelligence is production, and that these do not differ from each other in the Gods, but that with them to perceive intellectually and to make are the same thing, and that no other motion is necessary to the generation of things, but that they constitute all things by their very being or existence is manifested by these words" (the theme of the commentary).[207] Of those lesser gods called daemons we read, "If however the one Demiurgus imparts intellect to all things, there is likewise in these daemons, a certain ultimate vestige of the intellectual peculiarity, so far as they energize with facility according to imagina-

[207] *Proclus on the Timaeus,* Taylor, Vol. II, Bk. V, p. 373.

tion: for this is the last resounding echo, as it were, of intellect. Hence, the phantasy is said [by Aristotle] to be a passive intellect."[208]   Also we read that "The oracular Hermes or Thoth, declaring that nature creates by a kind of imagination, glorifies the world and man; makes man in this respect superior to the gods, that he has two sources, the intellectual and the animal or sensitive."[209]

It is, however, in Paracelsus that the imagination as a creative power is most glorified. Thus "The astral currents produced by the imagination and will of man produce certain states in external Nature, and these currents reach very far, because the power of the imagination reaches as far as thought can go."[210]   It is faith and imagination, says Paracelsus, which are the bases of magic processes and by them "we can accomplish whatever we desire. The true power of faith overcomes all the spirits of Nature, because it is a spiritual power, and spirit is higher than Nature."[211]   The "imagination is not *fancy,* which latter is the corner-stone of superstition and foolishness. The imagination of man becomes pregnant through desire, and gives birth to deed. . . . During sleep the sidereal man may by the power of the imagination be sent out of the physical form, at a distance to act for some purpose."[212]   "An imagination coming from a pure and intense desire of the heart acts instinctively and without any conscious effort. The power of a strong imagination directed upon another can kill or cure him according to the nature of the desire that impels the force, and which may be good or evil."[213]   "The great world is only a product of the imagination of the universal mind, and man is a little world of its own that imagines and creates by the power of imagina-

[208] *Ibid.,* Bk. IV, p. 304.
[209] *Macrobius,* Whittaker, p. 9.
[210] *Paracelsus,* Hartmann, p. 150.
[211] *Ibid.,* p. 149.
[212] *Ibid.,* p. 141.
[213] *Ibid.,* p. 161.

tion."[214] And, as a concluding instance, "If we only knew all the powers of the human heart, nothing would be impossible for us. The imagination is fortified and perfected through faith. . . . Faith must confirm the imagination, because it perfects the will."[215]

Paracelsus has much to say also of the Mumia, which he thus defines: "The Archaeus is the essence of life, but the principle in which this essence is contained, and which serves as its vehicle, is called Mumia. In the Mumia is great power, and the cures that have been performed by the use of the Mumia are natural, although they are very little understood by the vulgar, because they are the results of the action of invisible things, and that which is invisible does not exist for the comprehension of the ignorant. . . . The Mumia acts from one living being directly upon another, or it may be connected with some material and visible vehicle, and be employed in that shape."[216] And to these passages the translator and commentator, with what ancient or traditional authority does not appear, appends this note: "This invisible Mumia, that may be transferred from one living being to another, is nothing else but the vehicle of life, or 'animal magnetism.' "[217]

This is all curious lore and relevant to Shelley's conceptions in the *Witch*. She, too, creates mysteriously by some exercise of the imagination and affects the minds of human creatures through dreams. It would seem that the human imagination and will thus stimulated, if prompted also by desire, as in love, might create without bodily agency. "Women," says Paracelsus, "have a greater power of imagination during their dreams and when they are alone. . . . Women who are occupied a great deal with an evil imagination and who are

[214] *Ibid.*, p. 137.
[215] *Ibid.*, p. 162.
[216] *Ibid.*, pp. 185-87.
[217] *Ibid.*, p. 185, note.

unable to control it, should not be permitted to nurse and educate infants, because the impression which their imagination creates unconsciously impresses itself and acts injuriously upon the minds of the children."[218] Let me, by way of conclusion, add the opinion of Erasmus Darwin that "The similarity of the progeny to the parent, and the sex of it, are produced by the power of the imagination"[219]—a note to the lines:

> The potent wish in the productive hour
> Calls to its aid Imagination's power.
> —*Temple of Nature*, II, ll. 117-18.

I shall leave the reader to decide for himself how far Shelley subscribes to these beliefs, how great is his faith in the powers of imagination and in the operation of animal magnetism as a creative force even without the employment of a physical agency. The imagination toys with beliefs to which it but half subscribes. Perhaps, as Paracelsus declares, if it is backed by faith which animates the will it achieves that creative power which he conceives magic to be. It will suffice for our purposes to concede that Shelley, in the exercise of his imagination upon these ancient and mystical beliefs, employs the magic of his verse.

[218] *Ibid.*, pp. 159-60.   [219] *Temple of Nature*, p. 53.

CHAPTER IV

CONCLUSIONS

I⊤ HAS been necessary in this protracted argument upon the meaning of the *Witch* to cite copiously from various recondite authors. The interpretation I have advanced is new, and unless backed by a liberal array of evidence, is sure to arouse incredulity, especially amongst those lovers of Shelley who enjoy his flights of fancy and the richness of his imagery and yet have not perceived the character of his intellectual background nor known the strange foods upon which his imagination fed. For them I shall restate in simple terms, and briefly, the meaning of the *Witch of Atlas* as I conceive it to be.

The Witch is the daughter of Apollo and a sea nymph. She is the earthly embodiment of love, or Venus, who is the creative power of the universe. The Witch's realm is all beneath the moon, but her peculiar home, as Minerva, who is the intellectual aspect of Venus, is the air, which is between earth and heaven. In her spiritual rôle Minerva mediates between earth and heaven. She is intellectual beauty and the guide and inspiration of the human soul in its desire to return to its divine home, which is the realm of intellect, the archetypal world of ideas.

The Witch in her physical manifestations employs the intermediate form of the divine fire which is peculiarly resident in the atmosphere, electricity; but electricity is also magnetism, and magnetism is both a physical and a spiritual force. All forces, indeed, are twofold, physical and spiritual, and the electricity which is atmospheric fire is also love, for the divine fire of the ether, the ultimate creative principle of the universe, is also the divine love. Love, fire, electricity—these are but aspects of the universal principle which creates and animates all things. The Witch as creator and preserver of sublunary things employs these agents, love and electricity, for her purposes.

In her physical attributes the Witch is Isis, goddess of the moon, who presides over the rainfall and the dew and is worshipped as the goddess of fertility. The pagan meteorology had perceived the relation of sun and moon to the aerial phenomena which accompany the seasons, but it was not until the discoveries in electricity and chemistry during the latter half of the eighteenth century that the perpetual cycle of plant growth and atmospheric renovation was understood. Lavoisier discovered that water was composed of oxygen and hydrogen. These gases, released in the round of vegetable growth and decay, combined in the atmosphere to form water. The agent to their union was electricity; electricity, borne by the water vapor into the atmosphere, and the creator of clouds and rains, is the agent in the daily cycle of renovation and decay.

The Witch in her activities consistently supports this reading. She is the goddess of atmospheric phenomena, which move at the command of the electric fire. But she is also a spiritual force and as such her attributes are those of the earthly Venus, of Diana, and of Minerva as these symbols of divinity were interpreted by the neo-Platonists. Therefore is she the goddess of love, and of that intellectual beauty which informs the human soul of heavenly things, which manifests itself in dreams, and which as magnetism, a force both physical and spiritual, is the agency of healing. Those activities of the Witch which are not wholly physical are consistent with this interpretation of her powers, these being, both in a physical and spiritual sense, magnetic.

In this interpretation of the poem, which is supported by an array of evidence, as has been shown, there is no inherent obscurity. It is indeed simple provided the reader has familiarized himself with Egyptian myth, with neo-Platonism, and with the science of the latter eighteenth century. Perhaps "familiarize" is too strong a term. It suffices to have a sketchy knowledge of these subjects provided one can conceive what they meant to Shelley and the part which they played in his creative imagination. There, for most readers, lies, I think, the difficulty.

Shelley states that he was but three days in writing the *Witch of Atlas*. Inconceivable that he could invent the elaborate fable with its dual symbolism, physical and metaphysical, and dress it in poetic form in so short a time. Inconceivable certainly unless this symbolism, this whole body of thought, was so familiar to him that to employ it was as easy and natural as to compose in the language and symbol of the Christian philosophy and myth. Yet precisely thus it had become in the years of his poetic life. There are in *Queen Mab,* in *Alastor,* and in the *Revolt of Islam,* ideas and symbols employed in the same manner as in the *Witch.* And in *Prometheus* the philosophy, symbolism, and imagery are identical with those of the *Witch.*

I cannot here, it is obvious, demonstrate the extent and exactness of these parallels. Some few I have called attention to, and the complete scientific parallelism may be perceived by anyone who will compare the scientific lore of the *Witch* with the science employed in *Prometheus* as I have set it forth in *A Newton Among Poets.* The full correspondence of the neo-Platonism in the two poems I must here only assert. My later study of the *Witch* has confirmed, in this respect, my earlier study of *Prometheus.* The student has, indeed, to familiarize himself with Shelley's background and his habitual symbolism before either the *Witch* or *Prometheus* yields more than a superficial meaning. It is like learning a new language.

Has a poet, one may ask, the right to demand of his readers a new language if they would understand him? The answer is that Shelley asks nothing of the kind. He wrote *Prometheus,* as he says, for some five or six people, and the *Witch* he clearly wrote for his own amusement and to tease Mary Shelley. In the dedication of the poem he mocks Mary for her advice to write in a more popular and intelligible vein, one which the critics may approve. She is, he observes, "critic bitten," but he asserts his right to create for his own pleasure, to play with verse. And he challenges her to unveil his Witch. The poem and its challenge reveal her inability to understand him and his half-mocking acceptance of her inadequacy. That her inadequacy was complete is revealed in her comment on the poem, a comment which, unfortunately, later critics have taken at its face value, assuming that because she saw in the Witch no more than an exercise of fancy, there was no more to it than that. She writes—inanely to my thinking: "He loved to shelter himself . . . in the airiest flights of fancy, forgetting love and hate and regret and lost hope, in such imaginations as borrowed their hues from sunrise or sunset, from the yellow moonshine or paly twilight, from the aspect of the far ocean or the shadows of the woods," etc., etc. The wordy emptiness of much "aesthetic criticism" can offer nothing to surpass this.

The *Witch* has its meanings, right enough, and sufficiently difficult and complicated they are. If it be said that Shelley has no cause to complain if, when he writes in this fashion, he is not understod, the criticism is just. Yet it is evident that in the *Witch,* and to a less degree in *Prometheus,* Shelley had given up hope of an audience, and wrote, as few poets have ever written, to please himself alone. The reader who wishes to penetrate some way into the recesses of Shelley's thought and imagination has no recourse but to study Shelley's philosophic background and seek to learn the language of his symbols. Whether the results justify the labor each one must judge for himself. For myself the little I have learned has been exceedingly interesting and provocative and there are others, I believe, who will find the study equally so.

In the intimate revelation of a poet's creative processes there is a psychological interest above and apart from the value of his work as poetry. To the understanding of Shelley's mind, and of the poetic mind in general, an inquiry such as I have undertaken in *Prometheus* and the *Witch* is prerequisite. Shelley, as I conceive, has been very little understood these one hundred years; yet all good critics have had tantalizing glimpses of meanings hinted at, of depths unexplored behind his supposedly cloudy imaginings. The failure to get beneath the glittering surface of his profounder verse has been due, I believe, to the tradition—for which Mrs. Shelley is in part responsible—that he was a fanciful visionary, that he lived in a world of sensation and dream, that he was, in short, not an intellectual person. Yet a moment's thought should have revealed that he was one of the most intellectual of poets, for that part of his work which has been more or less understood from the first, his social criticism and philosophy, has its evident intellectual basis. Where his work has been in fields other than that of social and political philosophy, the obvious inquiry into his intellectual background, his knowledge of philosophy, neo-Platonism especially, has not been pursued.

It is easy to be wise after the event, and as I recall my own study of Shelley I perceive that I have been stupid in my failure to perceive the obvious. The hints were there, but I was blinded by the old traditional criticism and did not believe that Shelley was an intellectual poet. I was ignorant of neo-Platonism with its employment of symbols and its ration-

CONCLUSIONS 111

alization of myth. I was, more excusably, ignorant of the scientific thought of Shelley's time. Two suggestions led me to the studies I have undertaken and if anyone doubting my conclusions will pursue these suggestions wherever they may lead him I believe his findings will be similar to, if not identical with, my own. The one is Mr. A. N. Whitehead's assertion that Shelley's mind was as great in the field of scientific speculation as in poetry. The other is Mr. W. B. Yeats's surmise that Shelley's employment of the symbol of the cave derives from Porphyry. The clues to Shelley's background of science and neo-Platonism are there.

The *Witch of Atlas* is a playful composition but the symbols with which it plays are intellectual. To understand them we have had to resort to myth, to science, and to neo-Platonism. Shelley must have been very familiar with his materials to employ them so swiftly and so deftly. He must, for years, have read the neo-Platonists and the scientific philosophers of his own day. And from ideas thus derived he must have made the synthesis, the philosophy, which is evident in *Prometheus* and the *Witch*. We can, I think, plausibly trace his mental history to some extent and learn the workings of a mind unusual in its balance, a mind equally interested in social philosophy, in natural philosophy, and in metaphysics; a mind, too, desirous of attaining a unified and consistent picture of the universe.

In his earliest work his interest is in social reform and the discoveries of modern science which will aid mankind to a material Utopia. In *Alastor* we have postulated the conflict in his mind between the selfish pursuit of beauty and devotion to others. He seems to have feared for himself futility and destruction were he to permit his mystical and poetic instincts to dominate him. For, in the *Hymn to Intellectual Beauty*, also of the year 1816, Shelley recounts his mystical rapture and his dedication to the One, the source of goodness and beauty. The personal problem, therefore, is to reconcile in his own conduct the twin desires to reform the world and to pursue the life of poet and philosopher. The reconciliation I believe he found in a deeper study of neo-Platonism, which finds a place for man as artist and individualist and man as citizen in a world community. Metaphysically the problem is to reconcile multiplicity with unity.

Where, then, is the place of science in this unifying synthesis, for the dualism of mind and matter, like the dualism of multiplicity in unity, must in some way be resolved? Neo-Platonism denies reality to matter by pushing it to the vanishing edge of the universe and declaring it barely to escape non-being. Yet the dualism is not wholly avoided nor is the demonstration of neo-Platonism satisfying. It flatly asserts what, indeed, may be true but is left unproved. To the scientist working with matter it does not suffice merely to declare the non-reality of matter. If matter is a creation only of thought, if its existence is dependent wholly on our belief in it, it remains curiously stubborn and refuses to be, so to speak, unthought.

I have elsewhere shown the metaphysical implications of Newton's thought.[1] His postulated ether is as immaterial as thought itself. It is force emanating from the ever flowing spring which is God. This force, manifesting itself in light, electricity, magnetism, and all the energies of the physical universe, is, in its lowest manifestation, matter. Matter is the dregs, so to speak, of force. The resemblance of Newton's speculations to those of the neo-Platonists is evident, but his approach to the problem is different. Science does not deny the existence of matter but shows matter to be but one man-

[1] *A Newton Among Poets,* pp. 97-102.

ifestation of force. And force is something immaterial, something as intangible as thought or the spirit of animation.

From the time of Newton to the time of Davy, as I have elsewhere shown, the aim of one school of scientific thought was to resolve matter into force, into energy identical with, or akin to, spirit. This school, imaginative and speculative, was at odds with the materialists whose philosophy denied the existence of spirit, and these, as now, declared matter the only reality. But whether all matter is no more than immaterial force, or whether all force, thought, and animation are but adjuncts of matter, in either belief the antithesis is resolved to unity. The universe is wholly force, which, if you will, is thought; or it is wholly matter. Yet if we say force is matter or matter is force it will be seen that we differ only in our terminology and the positions of materialist and spiritualist are, in one respect, identical. So Shelley came to perceive, and whereas in his early writing he had been an avowed materialist, he later declares his indifference to the conflict of matter and spirit, perceiving it to be but a quarrel over terms.

Whether it be matter or spirit, the universe is none the less a varied spectacle, and to understand it the philosopher must demonstrate a unity underlying its diverse phenomena. To Newton the luminiferous or electric ether was the one divine energy fulfilling itself in many ways; and in the succeeding century, as the character of electricity was explored, to it were ascribed the powers of Newton's ether. It was thought to explain light, gravitation, and magnetic attraction. It was supposed to be identical with the spirit of animation and with animal magnetism. So, at least, it was regarded by imaginative scientists such as Darwin and Davy. That theories so far reaching were held by many or most of the scientists of the day to be unproved and fanciful may be guessed. Yet Shelley, it is apparent, subscribed to them, and his philosophy as set forth in *Prometheus* and the *Witch* is based upon them.

Their resemblance to neo-Platonic tenets is apparent and explains, I think, Shelley's acceptance of them. For neo-Platonism is in curious accord with the scientific theory of an electric universe. In neo-Platonism the divine love is a divine fire or ether from which the universe is fashioned. It is mind, it is soul, it is matter; in its triune character it manifests itself as the ethereal fire, as the fire of the upper atmosphere, and as the earthly fire which is the servant of man. Neo-Platonism, like myth and early science, seems here to anticipate the scientific discoveries of a later age.

It is possible, then, as Shelley has done, to weld neo-Platonism with certain of the scientific speculations of his day; to reinterpret the ancient myths in the spirit of neo-Platonism but with a more modern science. This he has done in *Prometheus* and the *Witch*. The symbols which he employs are those of neo-Platonism, but he endows them with a richer connotation, for the advances in the world's thought, in science especially, permit him so to do. Thus Isis or Minerva, manifesting herself in the upper air and precipitating the dews, becomes in the latest meteorology the goddess of atmospheric electricity. This is not inconsistent with the old myths nor with the neo-Platonic interpretation of them. It is merely an expansion, an elaboration of them.

Is this symbolism which Shelley employs in *Prometheus* and the *Witch,* expanding and enriching it with the connotations of science, merely a poetic language which provides him with the necessary dress for abstract but fanciful speculation? Or does the language of symbol conceal a genuine conviction, a philosophy which has unified the physical and the spiritual universe and in which he believes? In an interpretation of Shelley's creative life, in the effort to trace the growth of his mind, we must raise the question and endeavor to answer it; though it is one which does not, I think, permit of any certain solution. The *Witch,* moreover, by its very character, its whimsicality, is a poem which it would seem pedantic to take over-seriously, reading into it a declaration of belief.

I am denied here the results of an unpublished study of *Prometheus,* for to restate them would be to rewrite the book. I may only anticipate their evidence and assert that in *Prometheus,* which is most serious and which no one can think to be other than it is, the expression of Shelley's complete faith and philosophy—in *Prometheus* the symbolism is precisely that of the *Witch* and his beliefs the same. The *Witch* does not seek to answer the riddle of the universe. It plays lightly with the symbols of matter and spirit, but the ease of its recondite language and its very playfulness suggest one at home in a universe strange and unintelligible to others. It is only the adept who can play with the symbols of his faith, only the believer who can joke with God.

Belief may not be absolute, however, but provisional, tentative. Is it not possible that Shelley erected a speculative philosophy, a theoretical universe which supplied him with a language suited to his poetic genius but which was hardly more than a cloudland of theory? It is sufficiently evident that in his earliest productive years he was agnostic and materialistic in his attitude, and there is no evidence, despite his growing admiration for Christ and Christ's ethics, that he was ever in any orthodox sense a Christian or accepted any body of theological doctrine. He remains to the last, a sceptical, an agnostic intellect as his prose reveals. How then can we suppose him to accept the no less difficult theology of neo-Platonism or the universe of his creation which combines that philosophy with science? This would seem to many to be swallowing the camel.

The proof of belief is the willingness to act, and the state of a man's mind is shown by his habitual thought. Perhaps it would be unfair to stress too much the incident which tells of Shelley, while rowing Jane Williams on the bay, suggesting that they test the truth of Plato's belief in the hereafter. Perhaps the incident is exaggerated, or perhaps it is an instance of Shelley's humor, which was not of the best. Yet the anecdote illustrates what so much of his later verse supports, his preoccupation with the world of Platonic thought and his impatience, which his biographers reveal, with this imperfect world of sense. The carelessness with which he held his life, his desire to put the great mystery to the proof, suggest a man whose values are not those of ordinary men. Was he sane, then? Or had he become the victim of his own too great imagination, which in its insufferable picture of the world's agony, an agony he was impotent to assuage, drove him into the cloudy haven of his creation: a world of symbols clothing intellectual ideas, to be sure, not an irrational world of sensation and fancy; yet withal a refuge from the actual world of men?

There are various anecdotes which prove Shelley's imaginative susceptibility, the ease with which he abstracted himself from the immediate world of sense. These are natural to one with great powers both of imagination and thought. But in the last year or two of his life there occur other episodes of a curious character. There is the incident in which Shelley was seen to pass through the garden, whilst, as it was proved, being elsewhere at the time; the instance of his confronting his own apparition; the instance of the wraith of Byron's dead child, Allegra, calling to Shelley from the waves. There is Shelley's prescience of his death by drowning. What is to be made of such facts, or alleged facts, curiously coincident if invented? Is Shelley in the last months of his life sane or is he, as some would say, psychic?

In raising these questions I am seeking to face the facts so far as these are known, and to give my interpretation of them. There is no certain answer to some, for our tests of sanity, or of normality even, are not such as we can all accept without demur. In the case of a man of exceptional powers, such as was Shelley, it is meaningless to impose tests adapted to the average of the human race. The average human being, of no great imagination or intellect, lives in the world of the five senses and denies the existence of anything beyond them. All else is unreality, fancy, hallucination, and those who profess supersensuous experience are at the best queer and at the worst mad. Yet it is evident enough that men of unusual mental and imaginative powers have had unusual and inexplicable experiences. The neo-Platonic philosophers of Shelley's study record the familiar experiences of mystics, the rapturous union with the One. What is to be thought of these? Yet these philosophers are men of profound and subtle intellect and anyone who dismisses them as irrational, as in any way mentally inadequate, is not familiar with them. Or what shall be said of Swedenborg, notable scientist and thinker, whose powers of television are on record? And we have in our own time the recorded experiences of Mr. W. B. Yeats and "A. E.," strange as any told by the neo-Platonists or by the biographers of Shelley.

Genius, the commonsense of mankind affirms, is akin to madness. Men of great powers are subject to great aberrations. Therefore we dismiss in them what we do not understand. It is a comfortable way of avoiding difficulties, akin to the ways of psychologists who dismiss all psychical experiences which they cannot explain as hallucinations, delusions, or whatever the fashionable current word may be to designate what is not understood. Mesmer and his magnetic trance, which Shelley had himself experienced, was denounced by the medicine men, his rivals, as a charlatan, his discoveries a fraud; and nearly a century was to pass before his methods were rediscovered and given some scientific standing. The instance is not unique; is, indeed, typical. And the moral to be drawn is evident: it is unsafe to discredit the "abnormal" experiences of exceptional men. It is possible that as they exceed us in the exercise of powers which we know and understand, they exceed us in powers which we wholly lack. They may possess some sixth sense denied us.

It will be conceded that Shelley was a man of extraordinary intellectual and imaginative powers, widely read in many fields, science, poetry, and philosophy among them. He was capable of great powers of abstraction, could so immerse himself in thought as to be insensible, for long periods, to his surroundings. More than most men he lived in the world of ideas. And yet, more than most men, he was sensitive to the sufferings of mankind and in his earlier years devoted himself to the alleviation of them. Until he departed for Italy in the spring of 1818 Shelley was primarily a reformer and his pen was the instrument to his purpose. *The Revolt of Islam,* which he wrote when under seeming sentence of death, was his last despairing effort to give permanence to those ideas which he felt might reform the world and improve the lot of man.

The Italian years, the last phase, are the years of his great poetry. He is no longer the reformer employing his pen for didactic purposes, but a philosopher-poet whose theme is man in a disharmonious universe. Man's salvation and happiness no longer depend upon institutional reforms but upon his moral regeneration, his ability to comprehend the evil in his nature and by overcoming it to destroy the evil in the universe. This is the theme of *Prometheus*. The poem is not didactic but philosophic. It is not directed to an audience but answers for the poet's own satisfaction the questions which he put the universe. As he was a poet, a creator, he dressed this philosophical inquiry, this debate with his own soul, in poetic imagery. He employs symbols derived from the neo-Platonic philosophy, for these lend themselves to the poetic method, which suggests by its sensuous images the abstractions of philosophic thought.

It is an odd fact, however, that although this world of Shelley's thought is more abstract than the world of the *Revolt of Islam,* and the use of symbol more pervasive and subtle, it is yet more definite, more essentially "real." The *Revolt of Islam,* for all its conflicts and reforms and the actual geography of its scene, is in a vague and unreal world. Its propaganda and preachments do not rouse our interest, and the fate of its hero and heroine do not stir our emotions; whereas Prometheus, and Asia, Panthea and Demogorgon, and the Witch even, personification of aerial force and kindred powers, are real, are persons as well as abstractions. Whatever we may believe Shelley's mental state to be as he draws more within himself, we must recognize his growth in power, the greater clarity of his thought. We must observe, too, an unexpected skill in creating characters, as in the *Cenci,* and greater definiteness in his depiction of external nature. As he grows in mental power and his mastery of abstractions, the greater is his grasp of this world of ours, the world of sense and actuality.

We cannot easily, then, reconcile this manifest growth in power and clarity of thought with any theory of mental deficiency. If Shelley was ever "mad" he is demonstrably less mad in his later years than before, comprehending more clearly the nature of the sensible world even while he withdraws more and more into the world of his imagination. Our current psychology has plenty of pathological terms to characterize this withdrawal. It is presumably a confession of defeat; the imagination finds satisfactions which experience denies. Yet if the condition is pathological it should be accompanied by a weakened grasp on actuality, a growing inability "to face life." Such inability precisely does not characterize it, as I have pointed out, and I believe anyone well acquainted with Shelley's writings, prose and verse, will support me in my contention. The world of Shelley's thought in *Prometheus* and the *Witch* may be a difficult one to enter and understand, for reasons given, but it is a saner world, a more "real" world than that of *Queen Mab,* or *Alastor,* or the *Revolt of Islam.*

Protracted argument on the point is unprofitable, for the proofs of my contention are largely subjective, a matter of individual taste and judgment. There is implied, too, a seeming paradox: that as the mind more clearly and powerfully creates the unseen world of its imagining, the more lucidly does it perceive the world of sense reality. It is the unimaginative mind that fails to see life as it is, and the profoundly imaginative mind, one not beguiled by the seductions and illusions of sense, that perceives the relation of the unseen world to the seen. True it is, surely, that to the great religious teachers, the philosophers, the mystics, and the poets we look for the meaning of life, and it is they who declare the inadequacy of the world of matter and sensation and the existence of an unseen reality. The "fallings from us, vanishings" of which Wordsworth writes are not peculiar to him. Tennyson in his fashion repeats the same experience, which if not universal is at any rate common. The mystics proclaim it, and could we recall the emotions of childhood we should know again those moments in which we doubted the world of sense as the ob-

jects of our vision seemed to dissolve before us, leaving the
mind shaken and intolerably alone. The poetic and creative
mind retains this power and is unafraid; or losing it, like
Wordsworth, laments its passing.

Such is the testimony of the poets, and this experience,
which I shall not endeavor to explain, I should relate to that
enlargement of the world in which dwells the poetic mind,
repeopling the empty universe with creations of its own.
Sanely to hold the two in balance, the world of sense reality
and the imagined world of the unseen, is difficult and the
achievement only of the best minds. But the imagined world
of Shakespeare seems as real to us as the world in which we
live, and it interprets this world to us. The very different world
of Shelley's imagining is, when we can find our way into it, no
less substantial and logical and, too, with its revelations for
us in the realm of the familiar. To perceive in the phenomena
of the visible world the manifestation of invisible forces, and
in the cycle of the regeneration and decay of matter the symbol of the soul in its round of incarnations, is to have opened
to our sight a breath-taking universe. The experience here is
not one necessarily "believed" in the narrow theological sense.
We may or may not believe in soul at all, or its survival, or its
eternity, but the imagination liberated in a world conceived on
this hypothesis brings to the interpretation of experience a new
key which may or may not, individually, unlock for us the
door we seek. All logically imagined worlds are patterns
which give meaning and design to what, otherwise, is meaningless.

The pattern of Shelley's imagined world, however unusual,
is, as shown in the *Witch of Atlas* and *Prometheus,* extra-
ordinarily logical and consistent. For every force and phenomenon in the material world it seeks a spiritual counterpart,
the two being mutually interpretative. Thus the correspond-

ences noted between the spiritual force of love and the physical force of fire. The physical magnetism of the earth has its corresponding animal magnetism, which is psychical in its effect, though projected by physical means. The reader will earlier have observed in the dual use of the word "magnetism" a verbal fallacy. The magnetism of the earth, which is akin to electricity, is assumed to be the same as the force which induces the magnetic sleep or trance. This it may be said is sheer juggling of words. To two manifestations of force, both mysterious, we give the same name and then assume their identity. The assumption, be it said, is not originally Shelley's but is to be found in the speculation of his day for which I have advanced sufficient evidence. Yet Shelley would have been the first to detect the logical fallacy as such and his employment of magnetic attraction in the dual sense we have noted has then to be accounted for on other grounds than logical incapacity.

The terms, if you please, are a matter of convenience only, the idiom of the day with which Shelley was familiar. If speculation sought to identify the mysterious spirit of animation with the luminiferous ether, electricity with magnetism, magnetism with the strange phenomenon which we know as hypnotism, but which was then called "animal magnetism," the one fact of importance in all is not the terminology but the effort to reduce to a common basis, to unify, force, whether physical or psychical, in divers manifestations. The philosopher in his effort to compose this unity out of the multiplicity of details which constitute the dual universe of mind and matter need not quarrel with the terms. If all forces are the manifestations of the one force, they may be called love, electricity, or magnetism as suits our convenience. Their identity is accepted and interest lies in the variety of their expression and the correspondence between things physical and things psychical, the two being, it is assumed, different only in seeming, matter and spirit being one and the same.

What reality emerges from such speculations, such assumption of unity in multiplicity and the reduction of the phenomenal universe, of the material and psychical worlds, to the mysterious ether? Mind only. Nothing is sure but the individual mind in which exist these thoughts, and, by enlargement, the divine mind comprehending all lesser minds. Davy, drinking nitrous oxide, exclaims that "nothing exists but thought." The experiments with the ether trance tell the same story. Shelley, it may be, either from nitrous oxide or in the magnetic trance, knew emotionally the same experience. Intellectually it is the teaching of neo-Platonism and of the mysticism of the East. Did Shelley believe it or did he hold it tentatively, an hypothesis only? The evidence lies in his poetry, in the world of his imagining which he built upon this basis. That is a complex world, logically worked out, and consistent with itself. Its complexity proves this much, that Shelley had spent years in its elaboration and had become at home therein. In his absorption in it, in the evolution of his thought from materialism to mysticism, is manifest a measure of belief. This pattern of the universe which he built for his interpretation of experience was that which, in the years 1818-1820, as shown in *Prometheus* and the *Witch of Atlas,* best satisfied him in the maturity of his thought. The later poems, as I read them, strengthen this conclusion.

APPENDIX A

RALPH CUDWORTH

THE investigator pursuing the tortuous track of neo-Platonic ideas and symbols discovers with joy the works of Cudworth, seventeenth century Platonist. Like those isles of the blessed and the intelligible which Carlyle too seldom glimpsed in the flood of Coleridge's eloquence, Cudworth's *The True Intellectual System of the Universe* makes plain to the unmetaphysical mind what elsewhere is all too obscure. If indeed one first reads Cudworth, Thomas Taylor of a later time may be in part understood. It was Cudworth's object to demonstrate the essential monotheism of the best pagan philosophers. Behind the myths of Egypt and Greece, behind the gods and goddesses was, he declared, the One, the incorporeal and invisible God of whom each pagan deity was but an aspect, a visible symbol. This God he seeks evidently to identify with the Christian God, to blend a pantheistic Platonism with Christianity. And to my mind in his synthesis he achieves a lucidity and charm which is kindred to Shelley's in *Prometheus* and in the *Witch of Atlas*. That Shelley knew Cudworth I have no evidence, though it is not improbable. That Cudworth's neo-Platonism illuminates Shelley's thought will appear.

In a brief exposition of Cudworth's argument I can hardly do better than piece together passages from his work. They are intelligible without a gloss. To begin, then, with his definition of deity as conceived by the neo-Platonists: "Again, the supreme God is sometimes called by them . . . that intellectual principle, which contains the whole, as in this instruction of M. Antonius, . . . that, as our bodies breathe the common air, so should our souls suck and draw in vital breath from that great Mind, that comprehends the universe, becoming as it were one spirit with the same. . . . He is also called by them . . . the mind and understanding of the whole world . . . one intellectual fountain of all things."[1]

"God, who is, and is called the first Cause, is alone the fountain and original of all things, that are or seem to be; he by his superabundant fecundity produced from himself mind, which mind, as it looks upward towards its father, bears the perfect resemblance of its author, but as it looked downward, produced soul. And this soul again, as to its superior part, resembles that

[1] Ralph Cudworth, *The True Intellectual System of the Universe*, II, 343-44.

mind, from whence it was begotten; but working downwards, produced the corporeal fabric, and acteth upon body."[2]   And again: "It is plain, that, in the poetic theology, the Stoics took it for granted, that the natures of things were personated and deified, and that those gods were not animal, nor indeed philosophical, but fictitious, and nothing but the things of nature allegorized. Origen also gives us a taste of Chrysippus's thus allegorizing . . . that matter having received the spermatic reasons of God, containeth them within itself for the adorning of the whole world; and that Juno, in this picture in Samos, signifies Matter, and Jupiter God."[3]

"Timaeus Locrus asserted one eternal and unmade God, the maker of the whole world, and besides this, another generated god, the world itself animated, with its several parts . . . that eternal God, who is the prince, original, and parent of all these things, is seen only by the mind; but the other generated god is visible to our eyes, viz. this world, and those parts of it which are heavenly;—that is, the stars, as so many particular gods contained in it.   But here it is to be observed, that the eternal God is not only so called by Timaeus, as being without beginning, but also as having a distinct kind of duration from that of time, which is properly called Aeon, or Eternity, he therein follows Parmenides. . . . Time is but an image of that unmade duration, which we call eternity: wherefore, as this sensible world was made according to that exemplar or pattern of the intelligible world, so was time made together with the world, as an imitation of eternity."[4]

"We say, therefore, that there are several orders, ranks, or degrees of Zeus or Jupiter in Plato: for sometimes he is taken for the Demiurgus or opificer of the world, as in Cratylus; sometimes for the first of the Saturnian triad, as in Gorgias; sometimes for the superior Soul of the world, as in Phaedrus; and, lastly, sometimes for the lower soul of the heaven."[5]   And as for the lesser gods: "He [Apuleius] with Julian and others reduce the greater part of the Pagan gods to these ideas of the intelligible, or archetypal world, as making Apollo, for example, to be the intelligible sun, the idea of the sensible; and Diana the intelligible moon, and the like for the rest.   Lastly, it hath been observed also, that the

[2] *Ibid.*, p. 404.   [3] *Ibid.*, p. 513.

[4] *Ibid.*, pp. 277-78.   Compare, in *Prometheus Unbound*, "Thetis bright image of eternity," symbolizing Jupiter's attempt to extend, in his marriage with Thetis, his reign throughout time.

[5] *Ibid.*, I, 532.

APPENDICES — page 126

Egyptian theologers pretended, in like manner, to worship these intelligible gods, or eternal ideas, in their religious animals, as symbols of them."[6]

"According to the Pagan theology, God was conceived to be diffused throughout the whole world, to permeate and pervade all things, to exist in all things, and intimately to act all things. Thus we observed before out of Horus Apollo, that the Egyptian theologers conceived of God, as . . . a spirit pervading the whole world . . . which same theology was universally entertained also amongst the Greeks."[7] "And thus have we already shewed, that the more high-flown and Platonic Pagans . . . understood these consentes and select gods, and all the other invisible ones, to be really nothing else but the ideas of the intelligible and archetypal world (which is the Divine Intellect) . . . these gods . . . but several names and notions of the one supreme Deity, according to the various manifestations of its power in the world."[8]

"Nature is the last of all causes, that fabricate this corporeal and sensible world. . . . In proceeding . . . from that supreme goddess, the Divine wisdom, which is the fountain of all life, as well intellectual, as that which is concrete with matter. . . . And thus does the oracle describe nature, as presiding over the whole corporeal world, and perpetually turning round the heavens. . . . He [Proclus] saith the bodies of the sun, moon, and stars, supposed to be animated, were called gods too, they being the statues of the gods. . . . Nature is a god or goddess, not as having godship properly belonging to it, but as the Divine bodies are called gods, because they are statues of the gods."[9]

It follows from this all pervasive dualism of the archetype and its material image that love, personified in Venus, is twofold. "Hesiod's love was . . . the heavenly love, which is also God; that other love, that was born of Venus, being junior."[10] Urania Aphrodite, or the heavenly Venus, is but another name for God as comprehending the whole world. "Thus Pausanias in Plato's Symposium. . . . There are two Venuses, and therefore two Loves; one the older and without a mother, the daughter of Uranus or heaven, which we call the heavenly Venus; another younger, begotten from Jupiter and Dione, which we call the vulgar Venus: and accordingly are there of necessity two Loves, answering to these two Venuses, the one vulgar and the other heavenly.—The elder of these two Venuses is . . . the first be-

[6] *Ibid.*, III, 47-48.
[7] *Ibid.*, II, 497.
[8] *Ibid.*, p. 495.
[9] *Ibid.*, III, 312-13.
[10] *Ibid.*, I, 438.

getter of all . . . called by the Oriental nations Mylitta or Genitrix as being the fruitful mother of all . . . the first fair;—the cause of all pulchritude, order and harmony, in the world . . . Urania, or the heavenly Venus, was so called . . . because the love belonging to it was pure, and free from all corporeal affection:—which, as it is in men, is but a participation of that first Urania, or heavenly Venus and Love, God himself."[11]

"This heavenly Venus, which they affirm to have been begotten from Saturn, that is, from a perfect mind or intellect, must needs be that most divine soul (the third archical hypostasis) which being immediately begotten, pure from that which is pure, always remains above. . . . After which he speaks of another soul of the world, which is not separate from it, but closely conjoined therewith, he calling it a lower Venus and Love; namely, that other Venus, which in the fable is said to have been begotten from Jupiter himself (the superior soul of the world) and Dione, a watery nymph."[12]

Of the attributes and activities of Venus her presiding over copulation and childbirth is chief. "In like manner, they [the Greeks] called both the child-bearing of women and the goddesses that superintend over the same, Eilithyia, or Lucina; Coitus, or copulation, and the deity presiding over it, Aphrodite or Venus."[13] Her names, in accord with her attributes, are various: "Venus is either the moon, or Lucifer, or Hesperus."[14] These are her material or earthly aspects only, for, "Neither was Venus, according to this philosophic and arcane theology, taken only for the moon, or for Lucifer, or Hesperus . . . but, as we have already proved, for the supreme Deity also, either according to its universal notion, or some particular consideration thereof."[15]

Isis, or the moon-goddess, goddess of nature, is a name also for all the visible world and the creative powers which lie behind it: "That nature, which was the parent of things; the mistress of all the elements; the beginning and original of ages; the sum of all the divine powers; the queen of the seas; the first of the celestial inhabitants; the uniform face of gods and goddesses; which with my becks dispense the luminous heights of the heavens, the wholesome blasts of the sea, and the deplorable silences of hell; whose only divine power the whole world worships and adores, in a multiform manner, and under different rites and names.—From which words it is plain, that this goddess Isis was

[11] *Ibid.*, II, 466-67.
[12] *Ibid.*, III, 94-95.
[13] *Ibid.*, I, 473.
[14] *Ibid.*, II, 483.
[15] *Ibid.*, p. 484.

not the mere animated moon (which was rather a symbol of her) but that she was an universal Deity, comprehensive of the whole nature of things; the one supreme God, worshipped by the Pagans under several names, and with different rites."[16]

A being so various, with powers so multiform, is difficult to comprehend, so protean are her forms.   Thus usually she is identified with the moon, yet also is she sea-born Venus and yet again is she identified with the earth.[17]   She is knowledge, at war with Typhon, who is ignorance and error.[18]   She is veiled, as one having a visible or corporeal being, "and also something hidden and recondite; the sense seeming to be this: I am all that was, is, and shall be; and the whole world is nothing but myself veiled; but my naked and unveiled brightness no mortal could ever yet behold or comprehend."[19]   It is a passage which inevitably recalls the lines in *Prometheus Unbound* wherein Asia the earthly Venus becomes in her celestial apotheosis too bright for mortal eyes:

> Child of Light! thy limbs are burning
> Through the vest which seems to hide them.
> —*P. U.* II, 5, ll. 54-55.

In this diviner form Venus, the celestial love, is identifiable with Minerva, goddess of mind or intellect, "the only immediate offspring of the only maker and king of all things; for he had none of equal honour with himself, upon whom he should beget her, and therefore retiring into himself, he begot her and brought her forth from himself: so that this is the only genuine offspring of the first father of all."[20]

And as Isis or Venus is to be thought of in her dual aspect, her earthly and her celestial being, as matter and as mind, so likewise is Pan "not the corporeal world alone but chiefly the intellectual ruler and governor of the same."[21]   He is not only the Lord of the woods, "but the Lord or dominator over all material substance.   And thus does Phornutus likewise describe the Pan of the other Greeks, not as the mere corporeal world, senseless and inanimate; but as having a rational and intellectual principle for the head of it, and presiding over it; that is, for God and the world both together, as one system; the world being but the efflux and emanation of their Deity."[22]   He is "not the corporeal world

[16] *Ibid.*, p. 189.
[17] *Ibid.*, p. 105.
[18] *Ibid.*, p. 199.
[19] *Ibid.*, p. 171.
[20] *Ibid.*, p. 464.
[21] *Ibid.*, p. 176.
[22] *Ibid.*, pp. 176-77.

inanimate, nor yet as endued with a senseless nature only, but as proceeding from an intellectual principle or Divine spirit, which framed it harmoniously; and as being still kept in tune, acted and governed by the same. Which therefore is said to be the universal pastor and shepherd of all mankind, and of the whole world."[23]

These citations will all but suffice for my purpose in this historical background. I wish only to call attention to a few of the symbols employed by the neo-Platonists as cited by Cudworth. A more complete and elaborate symbolism will appear in the discussion of Thomas Taylor and his reading of the Platonic tradition, but in Cudworth are mentioned a few widely employed and frequently to be found in Shelley. Thus the serpent is the hieroglyph of deity, "Because the serpent feeding as it were upon its own body, doth aptly signify, that all things generated in the world by Divine Providence are again resolved into him."[24] The cave symbol of the world in Plato's usage is associated also with Zoroaster who "first of all, as Eubulus testifieth, in the mountains adjoining to Persis, consecrated a native orbicular cave, adorned with flowers, and watered with fountains, to the honour of Mithras, the maker and father of all things: this cave being an image or symbol to him of the whole world, which was made by Mithras."[25] The use of the ship as the vehicle for daemons is also remarked,[26] as elsewhere we have noted its association with the gods Isis and Osiris.

[23] *Ibid.*, p. 456.
[24] *Ibid.*, p. 157.
[25] *Ibid.*, p. 57.
[26] *Ibid.*, I, 510-11.

APPENDIX B

THOMAS TAYLOR

That Shelley had read the admirable and lucid Cudworth is unsure, but that he was familiar with some of the innumerable works of Thomas Taylor we learn from Hogg's account of his and Shelley's reading while at Oxford. Taylor, translator of Plato and of many neo-Platonists, is a cloudy, wordy, and exasperating writer, but it is necessary for the student of Shelley to have some knowledge of Taylor's work, especially of his translations of and comments upon Proclus. It is in these that I have found the most information upon neo-Platonic symbolism such as Shelley employs in *Prometheus Unbound* and *The Witch of Atlas*.

The metaphysical system of Proclus as set forth by Taylor appears to be, in its larger aspects at least, little different from that of Plotinus. It is monotheistic. The source of all is the One: "He is the One, self-proceeding; and from him all things proceed.

> And in them he himself exerts his activity; no mortal
> Beholds Him, but he beholds all.
>
> . . . .
>
> From Zeus were all things produced. He is male, he is female;
> Zeus is the depth of the earth, the height of the starry heavens;
> He is the breath of all things, the force of untamed fire;
> The bottom of the sea; Sun, Moon, and Stars;
> Origin of all; King of all;
> One Power, one God, one Great Ruler.[1]

The One, source of all, is identical with *the good:* "The simply good, and the simply one are the same, uniting and at the same time benefiting beings."[2] All things proceed from this one cause, for nothing can be antecedent to the good. "The good indeed . . . is coördinated with the beautiful."[3] These are one and the same, abstract perfection, the unqualified absolutes whence spring all limited and created things. "Plato . . . celebrates the king of all things, and refers to him the cause of the whole of things beautiful and good. Who, therefore, is the king of all things, except the unical God who is exempt from all things, who pro-

[1] Thomas Taylor, *The Eleusinian and Bacchic Mysteries*, Appendix, pp. 238-39.
[2] *The Six Books of Proclus, the Platonic Successor, on the Theology of Plato* (trans. by Thomas Taylor), II, 310.
[3] *Ibid.*, I, 125.

duces all things from himself, and is the leader of all orders according to one cause?"[4]

The One, who is prior to the gods, is manifest as light giving color to the heavens. "Hence he [Plato] calls that heaven intellectual colour, and light. For the light proceeding from *the good* is [in the orders] above [the heaven] unknown and occult, abiding in the adyta of the Gods; but it shines forth in this order, and from being unapparent becomes manifest. Hence it is assimilated to colour, the offspring of light."[5] This light emanating from the invisible God and token of his being, the light of good, is antecedent to intelligence. "By no means, therefore, is the first good to be considered as the same with intellect, nor must it be admitted that the intelligible is more ancient than all the hyparxis of the whole of things, since it is . . . subordinate to the light proceeding from *the good*."[6]

The One, like the Christian Deity, is triune. The three hypostases of his being are the Good (or the Beautiful), the Intellect, and the Soul. In the Intellect are conceived those images or archetypes which, when endowed with soul, take on visible form as gods or men. The third hypostasis, that of Soul, is the creative aspect of deity which realizes the ideas of the intellective aspect, the mind and imagination of deity. This triune symbolism runs through the entire philosophy, explaining the gods in their various functions and the mixed attributes of the human soul.

The sun, visible source of life and perfection in the created universe, is analogous to the intellect of God; it is the offspring of *the good,* and the author of light. This light of the visible sun is "a symbol of intellectual essences, and unfolds to the universe that which is arcane in the Gods that are above the world."[7] The sun, therefore, is regarded as the residence of God, or the symbol of God. "To say that God dwells in the sun, gives us a magnificent idea both of that glorious luminary, and the deity who dwells enshrined, as it were, in dazzling splendor."[8] The lights which are discussed in the unfolding of the Platonic doctrine are, however, rather obscurely threefold. There is a divine, an intellectual, and a sensible light corresponding to the three aspects of deity itself. It suffices that they serve to relate the intelligible with the good, whether metaphysically or physically. Light, then, is symbolical of truth: "Sensible light, and intellectual truth, are analogous to superessential light."[9]

[4] *Ibid.*, p. 131.
[5] *Ibid.*, p. 249.
[6] *Ibid.*, p. 115.
[7] *Ibid.*, II, 47.
[8] *Ibid.*, I, Intro., p. xiii.
[9] *Ibid.*, II, 44.

It must be borne in mind constantly in all readings of neo-Platonism that the universe discussed is always a dualism, that for every actuality of the material universe there is a corresponding spiritual reality.   Thus the sun, emanating light, is the visible source of power, but the soul of the universe is invisible.   "And the body of the universe indeed, was generated visible; but the soul is invisible, participating of the rational energy and harmony, and pertaining to intelligibles and perpetual beings, being generated by the best of causes, the best of generated natures."[10]

The deities of the pagan mythology personify, then, or symbolize, powers of the invisible God, the One.   Saturn is the symbol of the second hypostasis of divinity, intellect: "Saturn, as we have already observed, is *pure* [intuitive] *intellect*."[11]   He is the leader of all intellectual life, "he nourishes souls."[12]   Saturn's place is between that of his father (the One) and Jupiter, the fabricator of the visible universe.   Rather confusingly here, Rhea, "the vivific Rhea," enters the hierarchy: "Both Plato and Orpheus assert that she is the mother of the demiurgus of wholes, but a divinity posterior to Saturn."[13]   By this I suppose Rhea to be the third aspect or hypostasis of the celestial trinity, and Jupiter, loosely symbolizing this aspect, more correctly is a correspondent power on the visible and terrestrial plane.   The fluid use of these gods in myth and the overlapping functions and powers ascribed to them indicate the ever-present confusion of the gods of the terrestrial and generated order with the celestial and uncreated gods, symbols of the unseen deity.

Rhea is characterized as one possessed of a "fontal nature, and a power unically comprehensive of the divisible rivers of life."[14]   She fills the world with prolific power and has the inevitable triune character and function of godhood.   Apparently she corresponds to the celestial Venus elsewhere met with and defined, goddess of nature, mother of the gods, the vivific power of the universe.   In the lower world the sea-born Venus is her terrene counterpart and symbol.   Jupiter, it is said, deriving intellect from Saturn derives soul from Rhea, who is the fountain of soul.[15]   Jupiter, then, the fabricator of the visible universe, is himself triune, symbol of the invisible Deity and deriving therefrom his powers.

[10] *The Commentaries of Proclus on the Timaeus of Plato* (trans. by Thomas Taylor), Vol. II, Bk. III, p. 153.

[11] Taylor, *Eleusinian and Bacchic Mysteries,* p. 165.

[12] *Proclus on the Theology of Plato,* Taylor, I, 329.

[13] *Ibid.,* p. 334.   [14] *Ibid.,* p. 335.   [15] *Ibid.,* p. 376.

For the gods, to think is to create. "The demiurgic intelligence is production . . . with them to perceive intellectually, and to make are the same thing."[16] It is so both in the celestial and the terrestrial spheres: "The sun who imitates his father through the visible fabrication, evidently yields to an eternal and invisible production."[17] The gods, like the hypostases of the One, vary in their function: "Some of them are essential and vivific . . . others of them are intellectual, and excite by their very being all secondary natures to the perfection of life . . . others are unical, or characterized by unity."[18] The planets and the fixed stars are gods and rulers: "The planets are *cosmocrators,* or governors of the world" . . . and "each of the planets is the leader of a multitude of animals, or of certain other things of this kind."[19]

The world, which is filled with deity, unfolds itself in time, for to the terrestrial world time is the shadow and image of eternity. Always there is this dualism of the eternal and the unseen, and the temporal and the seen which seeks to perfect itself in the likeness of the archetype; it is a world which evolves in emulation of an inner standard or pattern. This is the most pervasive of the neo-Platonic ideas, one which Taylor endlessly repeats and illustrates in his comments upon Proclus and the rest. The world and the celestial bodies are but statues of the intelligible gods.[20] Always there is the visible form and the invisible essence.

The "Earth herself therefore, being a divine animal, is also a plenitude of intellectual and psychical essences, and of immaterial powers."[21] Not only does she nourish our bodies "but from her own soul perfects ours. By her own intellect likewise, she excites the intellect which is in us."[22] For the intellect is the divine and undying principle in all forms of life, both in greater and lesser beings. And as it is perfected and made strong so does the animal more and more resemble its divine prototype and approach divinity. To man, in this striving for perfection, the earth is nurse and guide. For man himself is threefold, mind, soul, and body, and the mind must free itself from the shackles of body and of soul before it returns to its immortal source. "Prometheus . . . is considered as bringing celestial light into generation, or leading

---

[16] *Proclus on the Timaeus,* Taylor, Vol. II, Bk. V, p. 373.

[17] *Ibid.,* Bk. III, p. 1.

[18] *Proclus on the Theology of Plato,* Taylor, I, 48.

[19] *Proclus on the Timaeus,* Taylor, Vol. II, Bk. IV, p. 222.

[20] *Ibid.,* p. 179.

[21] *Ibid.,* p. 286.   [22] *Ibid.*

the soul into the body, or calling forth the divine illumination, the whole being ungenerated, into generated existence."[23]

In the neo-Platonic elucidation of myth there is, besides the ever-present dualism of the real and the actual, of the archetype and its material image, a triune conception of deity which is often very confusing: "Hence, we may perceive at one view, as I have elsewhere observed, why the sun in the Orphic hymns is called Jupiter, why Apollo is called Pan, and Bacchus the sun; and why the moon seems to be the same with Rhea, Ceres, Proserpine, Juno, Venus, etc. For from this theory it follows, that every sphere contains a Jupiter, Neptune, Vulcan, Vesta, Minerva, Mars, Ceres, Juno, Diana, Mercury, Venus, Apollo, and in short, every deity,—each sphere at the same time conferring on these Gods the peculiar characteristics of its nature; so that for instance, in the sun they possess a solar property; in the moon a lunar one; and so of the rest."[24]

Thus above the sun there is a triad of celestial Gods—Mars, Jupiter, and Saturn.[25] Each of these may also be thought of in a threefold aspect. Jupiter in the terrestrial sphere is god of the summits, Neptune god of cavernous places, and Pluto god of the places under the earth.[26] Likewise Rhea, who in the invisible world is the third of the hypostases of the One, becomes in the terrestrial world Ceres. Ceres having therein her trifold powers and functions is often known as Diana, Proserpine, and Minerva.[27] Ceres is sometimes also identified with Juno,[28] and, as will sufficiently appear, in her generative aspect, with Venus.

For the purpose of this inquiry it is redundant to pursue the bewildering complications of all the gods in their innumerable phases. The mythology of the *Witch of Atlas* centers, from the evidence of the lines, in the phenomena of the moon, of earthly vivific nature, and of the air. The mythology of these will have to do with Venus, Diana, Minerva and the attendant and synony-mous deities of these goddesses. In the neo-Platonic interpreta-tions by Taylor of myth and symbol are a number of passages which, I believe, have a bearing on Shelley's practice in the *Witch of Atlas*. To these, therefore, I shall confine my further citations.

"The divine Iamblichus . . . asserts . . . that Juno is the cause of power, connexion, plenitude, and life to all things. . . . But

[23] Taylor, *Eleusinian and Bacchic Mysteries,* p. 204.
[24] *Proclus on the Theology of Plato,* Taylor, II, 142, note.
[25] *Ibid.,* p. 159.   [27] *Ibid.,* p. 38.
[26] *Ibid.,* pp. 34-35.   [28] *Ibid.,* I, 337.

Theodorus . . . calls Jupiter the power that governs the upper region as far as to the air; but Juno the power who is allotted the aërial part of the world. . . . For Jupiter is the essential of the soul that subsists in a material habit . . . but Juno is the intellectual part of such a soul."[29] Again, "It is . . . necessary to consider Neptune and Apollo as the fabricators of the whole of generation. . . But Juno and Diana, as the suppliers of vivification, the former rationally, but the latter physically. Minerva and Mars, as the causes of the contrariety which pervades through both existence and life; the former, of that which is defined according to intellect; but the latter, of that which is more material and passive."[30]

Yet it is evident also that with a slightly altered emphasis the creative Juno is no other than "Venus, who is the cause of beauty to generated natures, which is an imitation of intelligible beauty. This goddess also is the source of the union of form with matter; connecting and comprehending the powers of all the elements; and her principal employment consists in beautifully illuminating the order, harmony, and communion of all mundane concerns. She likewise governs all the coördinations in the celestial world and the earth, binds them to each other, and perfects their generative progressions through a kindred conjunction."[31] And similarly: "The Demiurgus produced Venus, in order that she might beautifully illuminate all mundane natures, with order, harmony, and communion. And he also produced Love as her attendant, who is the unifying cause of wholes."[32]

The place of Venus is the moon, "which comprehends the sacred laws of nature, the cause of generation."[33] From it she directs and animates the sublunary world with the "sublunary fire, which coadministers the natures of all the elements, moves all things, and excites their productions."[34] She "is venerated by all the earth, in many characters, various rites, and different appellations."[35] She is known as Juno, Venus, Diana, Minerva, Ceres, Bellona, Hecate, and Isis—the "fountain-deity" of nature, the "exemplar of that nature which flourishes in the lunar orb, and

[29] *Proclus on the Timaeus,* Taylor, Vol. II, Bk. V, pp. 328-29.

[30] *Ibid.,* Vol. I, Bk. I, p. 66.

[31] *Proclus on the Theology of Plato,* Taylor, II, 143.

[32] *Proclus on the Timaeus,* Taylor, Vol. I, Bk. III, p. 431.

[33] *Ibid.,* Bk. I, p. 29.

[34] *Ibid.,* Vol. II, Bk. IV, p. 229.

[35] Taylor, *Eleusinian and Bacchic Mysteries,* p. 115.

throughout the material world, and from which the deity itself of the moon originally proceeds."[36]

The moon occupies an intermediary place between heaven and earth and has dominion over souls, which, analogously, are intermediary between mind and body in the triune conception of man. Not only is she the goddess of fertility and production, of love and marriage, but likewise she elevates the soul to communion with the highest, the intellectual, order of the universe. Thus "She likewise gives perfection to souls through a life according to virtue."[37] In the persistent dualism of the neo-Platonic philosophy the moon therefore is sometimes called a "celestial earth,"[38] for "Heaven is in Earth, and Earth in Heaven."[39] "The Pythagoreans however say, that the elements may be surveyed in the heavens in a twofold respect, in one way indeed prior to the sun, and in another after it: for the moon is ethereal earth."[40] It is from this all pervasive concept of the archetype and the material object, of moon and earth as soul and body, that the seeming confusion arises whereby Venus or Isis in her multitudinous avatars is spoken of sometimes as goddess of earth, sometimes as goddess of the moon.

The somewhat Delphic passage which I next cite associates the moon with the arts and artists: "The philosopher Porphyry however, in interpreting these things, supposes Vulcan to be the intellect that presides over art, but earth to be the lunar sphere. *For this is called by the Egyptians ethereal earth.* He says therefore that souls which derive their subsistence from divinity, but participate of the artificial [or Vulcanic] intellect, are disseminated in the body of the moon; souls that give themselves to the arts, dwelling there; and that they have bodies which are effluxions of the ethereal bodies."[41] The dual aspect of the moon is repeatedly emphasized, her terrestrial creative power and her spiritual influence whereby man is made acquainted with reality. Hence, no doubt, her association with the arts and the creative instinct in man. "The moon is the cause of nature to mortals, *and the self-revealing image of the fountain of nature.*"[42]

The moon, "the statue of fontal nature," typifies the mother of the gods and men; she is Venus; she is the ethereal earth, the dwelling place of souls who thence descend into mortal existence.

[36] *Ibid.*, p. 119.
[37] *Proclus on the Theology of Plato,* Taylor, II, 143.
[38] *Proclus on the Timaeus,* Taylor, Vol. II, Bk. V, p. 316.
[39] *Ibid.*, p. 315.
[40] *Ibid.*, Vol. I, Bk. III, p. 426.   [41] *Ibid.*, Bk. I, pp. 123-24.
[42] Taylor, *Eleusinian and Bacchic Mysteries,* p. 113.

In her manifold aspects she is known variously as Diana, Hecate, Proserpine, Ceres, Minerva. The last, Minerva, "is the monad of the triad which is there" [moon] and "the Egyptian says, that Minerva is allotted the city which is named after her, and also his own city Saïs."[43] With her are associated the "leaders of the mysteries in Eleusis . . . derived from Musaeus, the offspring of the Moon."[44] The associations of Minerva are intellectual, philosophic, "being brought forth indeed from the summit of her father, and abiding in him; being a demiurgic, separate, and immaterial intelligence."[45] Thus "by Minerva we must understand that original, intellectual, ruling, and providential deity, who guards and preserves all middle lives in an immutable condition, through intelligence and a self-supporting life, and by this means sustains them from the depredations and inroads of matter."[46]

Minerva, "being full of intellectual knowledge, and true wisdom," is philosophic and has her various hypostases, solar, lunar, and earthly. She is called "Core, as being a virgin, and as purifying from all conversion to externals."[47] She is associated with prudence and with divination,[48] and with the science of medicine. "Porphyry . . . says that medicine very properly proceeds from Minerva, because Esculapius is the lunar intellect, in the same manner as Apollo is the solar intellect."[49] Again "she is *Calliergos,* or the beautiful fabricator, as connecting by beauty all the works of the father; a *Virgin,* as exerting an undefiled and unmingled purity."[50]

The association of Minerva with an earthly dwelling place is appropriately the mountain of Atlas, which, highest of known mountains and supporting the heavens, is appropriate to the most intellectual of deities, one who springs from the highest part of the father, Zeus. "Hence too, poets establish the Demiurgus on the highest summit of the world; it being allotted so great an aptitude from him, to the participation of intelligible causes."[51] And again: "Such also is the Titanic order with the Gods to which Atlas belongs. And the first of these ten kings was called Atlas, and as is said in the Atlanticus gave the name of the island. The summits, therefore, of the second coördination, are adorned

[43] *Proclus on the Timaeus,* Taylor, Vol. I, Bk. I, p. 118.
[44] *Ibid.,* p. 139.   [45] *Ibid.*
[46] Taylor, *Eleusinian and Bacchic Mysteries,* p. 190.
[47] *Proclus on the Theology of Plato,* Taylor, II, 39.
[48] *Proclus on the Timaeus,* Taylor, Vol. I, Bk. I, pp. 133-34.
[49] *Ibid.,* p. 134.   [50] *Ibid.,* p. 142.
[51] *Ibid.,* Bk. III, p. 454.

indeed by the Olympian Gods, of whom Minerva is the leader. . . ."[52]

To Thomas Taylor all myths were symbolical both of theological and physical truths. He thus interprets the fable of Saturn devouring his children: "It insinuates nothing more than the nature of an intellectual (or intuitional) god; since every such intellect returns into itself."[53] Physically interpreted the same myth signifies Time devouring the parts of time which are "the children of the universe."[54] The merely physical interpretation Taylor condemns and speaks contemptuously of the "frigid and trifling interpretations of Bacon and other modern mythologists."[55] The physical interpretation is to him always secondary and trivial, "For the fables of the wise are about things of an eternal nature; but those of children about temporal things and which are of small consequence."[56] Plato has said of the Egyptians that they "obscurely signified the arcana of nature through fable."[57]

It is in this wise that Taylor interprets the fables of the "descent of Hercules, Ulysses, etc., into Hades and their speedy return from its dark abodes . . . 'Hercules being purified by *sacred initiations,* obtained at length a perfect establishment among the gods:' that is, well knowing the dreadful condition of his soul while in captivity to a corporeal nature, and purifying himself by practise of the cleansing virtues, of which certain purifications in the mystic ceremonies were symbolical, he at length was freed from the bondage of matter, and ascended beyond her reach. On this account, it is said of him, that

'He dragged the three-mouth'd dog to upper day';

intimating that by temperance, continence, and the other virtues, he drew upwards the intuitional, rational, and opinionative part of the soul."[58] And again he explains the regeneration of the soul under these terms: "She is bound in body Prometheiacally and Titanically: she frees herself therefore from its bonds by exercising the strength of Hercules; but she is collected into one through the assistance of Apollo and the savior Minerva, by philosophical discipline of mind and heart purifying the nature."[59]

[52] *Ibid.,* Bk. I, p. 153.
[53] Taylor, *Eleusinian and Bacchic Mysteries,* p. 131.
[54] *Ibid.*   [55] *Ibid.,* p. 80.
[56] *Proclus on the Timaeus,* Taylor, Vol. I, Bk. I, p. 106.
[57] *Ibid.,* p. 108.
[58] Taylor, *Eleusinian and Bacchic Mysteries,* pp. 75-76.
[59] *Ibid.,* pp. 99-100.

Virgil, Taylor thinks, had but a superficial knowledge of Platonism. He nevertheless finds symbolism in the *Aeneid,* as thus: " 'So, now, at the first beams and rising of the sun, the earth under the feet begins to rumble, the wooded hills to quake, and dogs were seen howling through the shade, as the goddess came hither,' " which Taylor thus interprets: "And the howling dogs are symbols of material demons, who are thus denominated by the *Magian Oracles* of Zoroaster, on account of their ferocious and malevolent dispositions, ever baneful to the felicity of the human soul. And hence Matter herself is represented by Synesius in his first *Hymn,* with great propriety and beauty, as barking at the soul with devouring rage. . . ."[60] Again of another passage he remarks: "Does it not afford a beautiful representation of a corporeal nature, of which a cave, defended with a black lake, and dark woods, is an obvious emblem? For it occultly reminds us of the ever-flowing and obscure condition of such a nature, which may be said

> To roll incessant with impetuous speed,
> Like some dark river, into Matter's sea."[61]

Of the symbols employed by Taylor in his interpretations, the fountain is among the chief. Proclus is thus cited as uttering in a dream these verses:

> High above aether there with radiance bright,
> A pure immortal splendor wings its flight;
> Whose beams divine with vivid force aspire,
> And leap resounding from a fount of fire.[62]

The fountain of ethereal fire springs from the One, symbolizing the mysterious source of all things; and fountain and fire are symbols constantly employed both of spiritual and material forces. So Ceres, or Rhea, is described as holding in her right hand "Juno the fountain of souls, and in her left Vesta the fountain of virtue."[63]

Fire is both celestial and sublunary: "For the fire which is in generation, is a certain effluxion of the celestial fire, and is in the cavities of the other elements; there not being a sphere of fire by itself; but the summits of air imitate the purity of the upper fire. We say therefore, that these summits are sublunary fire, and that the place of fire is under the heavens. . . . Truly-existing fire,

[60] *Ibid.,* pp. 54-55. [61] *Ibid.,* p. 53.
[62] *Proclus on the Theology of Plato,* Taylor, I. Intro., p. xlix.
[63] *Proclus on the Timaeus,* Taylor, Vol. II, Bk. III, p. 129, note.

therefore, is in the heavens. But the purest of sublunary fire is
in the air proximate to the heavenly bodies, which Plato farther
on, calls aether. And fire of the grossest nature is contained in
the bosom of the earth."[64] Fire is a symbol of divinity: "The
idea therefore, of that which is divine, he for the most part produced from fire, in order that it might be most splendid and
beautiful to the view."[65] Is it by reason of its association with
the divine energy of fire, therefore, that lightning becomes the
symbol of fabrication? "For thunder [i.e., lightning] is a symbol
of fabrication, proceeding through all things without contact, and
vivifying all things."[66]

"There are," says Taylor, "many divine fountains contained in
the essence of the demiurgus of the world; and . . . among these
there are three of a very distinguished rank, namely, the fountain
of souls, or Juno,—the fountain of virtues, or Minerva—and the
fountain of nature, or Diana. This last fountain too immediately
depends on the vivifying goddess Rhea. . . ."[67] The fountain,
then, symbolizes a source of creative energy: "The natures therefore, that are immortal from themselves, resemble the fountains
of water: but those that are filled from these, may be assimilated
to perpetually flowing rivers; and those that are sometimes vivified,
and sometimes lose their life, to rivers that cease to flow."[68]
And again: "A river is the symbol of life, and consequently signifies in this place [Virgil] the *intellectual or spiritual life, proceeding from on high,* that is, from divinity itself, and gliding
with prolific energy through the hidden and profound recesses of
the soul."[69]

If a river is a symbol of life, so *"The Nile also is a symbol of
the life which is poured on the whole world."*[70] A boat thus becomes naturally the vehicle for divinity and, by derivation, for the
soul set upon the voyage of mortality. Says Wilder in an annotation of a passage in Porphyry: "The one 'sailing in a Boat' sets before the mind the power that directs the world."[71] Water by
reason of its fluidity, its inconstancy, is, simply enough, a symbol
for matter: "The Egyptians," says Simplicius, "called matter,

[64] *Ibid.,* Bk. IV, pp. 264-65.

[65] *Ibid.,* p. 265.   [66] *Ibid.,* Vol. I, Bk. I, p. 94.

[67] Taylor, *Eleusinian and Bacchic Mysteries,* pp. 113-14.

[68] *Proclus on the Timaeus,* Taylor, Vol. II, Bk. V, p. 372.

[69] Taylor, *Eleusinian and Bacchic Mysteries,* p. 96.

[70] *Proclus on the Timaeus,* Taylor, Vol. I, Bk. I, p. 81.

[71] Iamblichos, *Theurgia,* Wilder, p. 241.

which they symbolically denominated water, the dregs or sediment of the first life; matter being, as it were, a certain mire or mud."[72]

The individual soul, a "dry fire," descending from heaven, puts on the vehicles of mortality, the lowest of which is symbolized by water, which is matter. As to the experiences of the soul upon death of the body and its ascent to its original source there are, according to Taylor, differences of opinion among the neo-Platonic philosophers regarding the fate of the soul's vehicles: "Porphyry and his followers, refuse indeed to admit this corruption, as it is called, which dissipates the vehicle and the irrational soul. . . . The words of Plato must be adduced, in which he evidently does not destroy the whole of the irrational nature. . . ."[73] "That he preserves the vehicle of the soul perpetual, is evident from his representing souls using their vehicles in Hades. For ascending into their vehicles, as Socrates says in the Phaedo, they pass over the river."[74] And again: "This life . . . is of longer duration than the life of the present body; and hence the soul when in Hades, and choosing different lives, has a life of this kind."[75] Earthly life is itself a symbol of Hades, or of Heaven: for if *he who in the present life is in subjection to his irrational part is truly in Hades, he who is superior to its dominion is likewise an inhabitant of a place totally different from Hades.*"[76]

It is the opinion of wise men, says Taylor, that Hell or death commences in this present life "and that, consequently, sense is nothing more than the energy of the dormant soul, and a perception, as it were, of the delusions of dreams."[77] It is "when purified from the defilements of a material nature, and constantly elevated to the realities of intellectual [spiritual] vision,"[78] that the soul realizes felicity. As to the state of the soul after death, the ancient theologists believed, said Ficinus, that divine things were *"the only realities, and that all others were only the images and shadows of truth."*[79] Thus the soul's after state was but "a continuation of its state at present, and a transmigration, as it were, from sleep to sleep, and from dream to dream."[80] Men without vigilance, without concern for divine things, should they happen to die in this sleep of earthly existence become "afflicted with similar and still more dazzling visions in a future state."

[72] Taylor, *Eleusinian and Bacchic Mysteries,* p. 44.
[73] *Proclus on the Timaeus,* Taylor, Vol. II, Bk. V, p. 365.
[74] *Ibid.,* p. 366.   [75] *Ibid.,* p. 367.
[76] Taylor, *Eleusinian and Bacchic Mysteries,* p. 88.
[77] *Ibid.,* pp. 80-81.   [79] *Ibid.,* p. 45.
[78] *Ibid.,* p. 87.   [80] *Ibid.,* p. 36.

Thus "he who in this life pursued realities, would, after death, enjoy the highest truth," but "he who pursued deceptions would hereafter be tormented with fallacies and delusions in the extreme: as the one would be delighted with true objects of enjoyment, so the other would be tormented with delusive semblances of reality."[81]

"The soul therefore *dies* as much as it is possible for the soul to die: *and the death to her is, while baptized or immersed in the present body, to descend into matter, and be wholly subjected by it; and after departing thence to lie there till it shall arise and turn its face away from the abhorrent filth. This is what is meant by the falling asleep in Hades, of those who have come there.*"[82] By these words are explained the statement of Plato, Taylor alleges, "that the unpurified soul in a future state lies immerged in mire."[83] Doctrines such as these were, however, only for the elect: "It would have been a ridiculous prostitution to disclose to the multitude a theory so abstracted and sublime. It was sufficient to instruct these in the doctrine of a future state of rewards and punishments, and in the means of returning to the principles from which they originally fell."[84] For, again, "Pythagoras confirms . . . 'that whatever we see when awake, is death; and when asleep, a dream.' "[85]

The excerpts I have made from Taylor may seem all too copious but they are indeed but a small part of those which might be quoted, with sufficient relevance, to create the background of neo-Platonic thought and symbol necessary to an understanding of the *Witch of Atlas*. Those familiar with the poem will have been already struck with the many similarities of Shelley's thought and imagery to these excerpts.

[81] *Ibid.*, pp. 45-46.
[82] *Ibid.*, pp. 38-39.
[83] *Ibid.*, p. 43.
[84] *Ibid.*, pp. 46-47.
[85] *Ibid.*, p. 38.

APPENDIX C

CLAUDE ÉTIENNE SAVARY

It is commonly assumed that Shelley derived the theme of *Ozymandias* from Diodorus Siculus, but he may with equal likelihood have derived it from Savary, who writes: "The colossus bears this inscription, *I am Osymandyas, king of kings: he who would comprehend my greatness, and where I rest, let him destroy some one of these works.*"[1] The letters of Savary are an instance of the revived interest in Egypt which marks the latter eighteenth and early nineteenth centuries. Savary is familiar with the ancient rationalization of myth and cites Plutarch and Macrobius. Cudworth also is alluded to but Savary seems to have had little interest in neo-Platonism and the metaphysical interpretations of myth. His bent is rational and scientific and the ancient fables to him are expressive of the solar myth. To the ancient rationalization he adds, however, a somewhat more modern note in accord with the contemporary interest of scientists in meteorological phenomena. I shall briefly summarize his recapitulations and stress those details which may be of especial interest to the present inquiry.

That the Egyptian priesthood disguised astronomical and other scientific lore in the form of fable for the understanding of the vulgar, Savary in several instances insists: "The initiated, and, particularly, the priests . . . did not believe that idolatry they taught the people; nay, it is reasonable to suppose, their first doctrine was that these luminous bodies [sun, moon, and stars] were the work of God."[2] Again: "In the sanctuaries of their temples the Egyptian priests secluded this sublime doctrine, either transmitted by the first men or imagined by their own genius; as by Abraham, from the efforts of reason, and the study of astronomy. Having enveloped them in allegories which themselves, only, could unfold, they left the people in total ignorance, favoured their idolatry, and, at the death of each individual, thus prayed: 'O Sun, and ye other gods, who bestow life, receive me; restore me to the eternal deities, that I may dwell with them.'"[3] The four ages of the sun and the seasons of the year were symbolically expressed by emblems representing a child, youth, mature man, and aged man.[4]

[1] Claude E. Savary, *Letters on Egypt,* II, 53.
[2] *Ibid.,* p. 324. [3] *Ibid.,* pp. 314-15. [4] *Ibid.,* p. 333.

The Egyptian symbols represent not only phases of the sun and moon but conditions peculiar to Egypt: the Khamsin, or destructive wind, deified as Typhon, often overcomes Osiris, the sun, in the early spring of the year. The evil wind is dissipated as the spring advances and Horus, the ascendant sun, triumphs. The Etesian, or cooling winds, dispelling vapours, then displace Typhon. "Naturalists, observing the influence of the moon on the atmosphere, allied her to the god [Horus] to chase the usurper from the throne."[5]

It will be needless, for our purposes, to pursue Savary's complete explanation of the Egyptian symbolism of myth. The various powers of Phtha, Neith, and Athor correspond to the hypostases of divinity in neo-Platonic theology. We may note in passing the hermaphroditic character of the creator: "The Egyptians, that they might give the Creator a sensible form, attributed two sexes to him."[6] The Egyptian deities have their correspondences, likewise, with the Grecian. Also, "Water is the principle of all things, and God the spirit which has formed the universe from this humid principle."[7] Phtha, the creative spirit, is "the most pure and subtle fire, above the ether."[8]

The aspect of deity which signifies wisdom, Neith, corresponds to the Minerva of the Greeks: "The priests of Egypt more particularly adored, in Neith, the divine wisdom which guides the world, and enlightens men, and made her the protector of the arts."[9] Osiris is likewise identified with Bacchus and also with the Nile, which is the preserver of Egypt.[10] Typhon, the deadly wind, is also the spirit of evil and it is interesting to note, in our inquiry into the meaning of symbols, that to Typhon are dedicated the crocodile and hippopotamus.[11]

Athor, aspect of deity, signifies "that mysterious Night which was over chaos, before the creation; afterward the Moon; and, lastly, Winter; by this analogy, the Orientals, Greeks and Romans, have named Athor Venus the Queen of the World, and the Mother of Delights."[12] Again: "Philosophers have honoured the upper hemisphere with the name of Venus, and the lower with that of Proserpine."[13] The goddess is represented as in tears, weeping the passing of the sun into the southern hemisphere.[14] She is also

[5] Ibid., p. 341.
[6] Ibid., p. 312.
[7] Ibid.
[8] Ibid., p. 315.
[9] Ibid., p. 318.
[10] Ibid., p. 325.
[11] Ibid., Letter XXXIV.
[12] Ibid., p. 308.
[13] Ibid., p. 307.
[14] Ibid.

identifiable with Diana,[15] and "she has great affinity with the Ceres of the Greeks."[16]

"Isis is the genius of the Nile. . . . They say the degrees of the elevation of the waters answer to the phases of the Moon."[17] It was observed by the priests of Egypt, says Savary, that the "Moon had an immediate influence on the atmosphere, wind, and rain."[18] To Bubastis, a phase of Isis and to be identified with her, "The Egyptians attributed . . . the virtue of succouring pregnant women. . . . The Greeks and Latins, disciples of the Egyptians, ascribed the same power to Diana."[19] The Moon is relevantly associated with the power of generation: "The priests pretend the Moon sheds a generative light."[20]

"Philosophers have called the upper atmosphere, a part of which we inhabit, Venus."[21] The association with fertility and with dew is evident: "The Egyptians were attentive observers, and divided the time between the New and Full Moon into three equal parts. The first was called the imperfect gift; and the third, from the 11th to the 15th, was dignified with the title of the perfect gift; because the dews then fell abundantly."[22] Upon the relation of dew to the phases of the moon Savary then speculates at length. I quote the more relevant passages in full, for I believe them to have significance in our interpretation of the *Witch of Atlas* and the identification of the Witch and her functions.

"Let us examine, for this is the true object of enquiry, what the priests meant. The phaenomena of nature was their peculiar study, which they uninterruptedly pursued under a climate much less variable than that of Europe. They learned to foresee, from the observations of ages, preserved in the sacred archives, what must happen at stated seasons. They had remarked that dew was not abundant at the New Moon, but exceedingly so at the full: they supposed the Moon greatly to influence the atmosphere, to attract vapours from lakes and rivers, and return them in dew; they, therefore, made the Full Moon a deity, which they named Butis. Agreeable to their principles, her abode was beside the grand lake, that she might more easily quench her thirst; which doctrine, come from Egypt, or where it will, or whether or not supposed by Philosophers to be well founded, has been adopted by many of the ancients and moderns.

[15] *Ibid.*, p. 305.
[16] *Ibid.*, p. 361.
[17] *Ibid.*, pp. 359-60.
[18] *Ibid.*, p. 357.
[19] *Ibid.*, p. 370.
[20] *Ibid.*, p. 389.
[21] *Ibid.*, p. 425.
[22] *Ibid.*, p. 379.

" 'The stoics say the Sun heats the waters of the sea with his rays, and the Moon attracts the mild humidity of lakes and fountains.'[23] Pliny says, 'Soft waters are the element of the Moon, and salt that of the sun.'[24] 'At the full of the Moon, the air dissolves in rain; or, if the sky is serene, distills abundant dews, which occasioned the lyric poet, Alcman, to call the dew the son of the Air and the Moon.'[25] Among modern Naturalists, M. Mile has adopted this opinion. 'In a fine day, and, especially, in Spring, a cold and subtle vapour is attracted by the Moon, into the middle region of the air; whence, soon condensed to imperceptible drops, it falls to the ground, in abundant dews, and yields the necessary nutriment to plants.'[26]

"No one can deny the Moon greatly to influence the atmosphere; but, I believe, it would be difficult to prove it attracts water. This is the property of the Sun, which, by expanding humid particles, renders them lighter than the air, through which they rise, till they find an equilibrium. But were the ancients ignorant of this attraction, or do not the cited passages tend to prove they were not, and that they knew it was greater when the Sun and Moon were in opposition? Whether or not, the Egyptians, living in a hot climate, seldom refreshed by the salutary rains common to others, and which would be uninhabitable did not night dews give life to vegetables, carefully observed how they were produced; and, perceiving them heaviest at the Full Moon, created a presiding deity. 'Dew falls most abundantly at the full of the Moon.' "[27]

[23] *Ibid.*, pp. 376-78, quotation from Plutarch.
[24] *Ibid.*, quotation from Pliny, lib. 2.
[25] *Ibid.*, quotation from Macrobius, *Saturnalia,* lib. 7.
[26] *Ibid.*, quotation from Mile, *Hist. Nat.,* tom. 2.
[27] *Ibid.*, quotation from Plutarch.

APPENDIX D

ERASMUS DARWIN

In Erasmus Darwin's extensive notes to *The Botanic Garden* and *The Temple of Nature* are several allusions to mythology, which Darwin rationalizes in terms of chemical and biological science. The importance of Darwin's notes is twofold: not only does he interpret myth in more explicit scientific terms than do the writers thus far cited, but also it is probable his example suggested to Shelley similar processes of rationalization and the like use of poetic symbol. Darwin's influence is early evident on Shelley, as *Queen Mab* attests, and as allusions in letters to Elizabeth Hitchener further support. Darwin's references to Bacon would, of course, open up the field, and any early reading by Shelley of Thomas Taylor's works would supplement the physical rationalization with the metaphysical. Or, what is probable, the dual interpretation to be found in Plutarch's *Of Isis and Osiris* would open the way for Shelley both to the rationalists and the mystics. Plutarch and Darwin are the most likely starting points, then, for Shelley's study and rationalization of myth and for its symbolical use in verse; and of the two Darwin is the more certain on the score of evidence and probably the earlier, Shelley's acquaintance with him being not later than 1811.

Darwin's allusions to the allegories of myth repeat themselves somewhat and may be briefly summarized. The old mythologies veiled, he believed, the scientific knowledge of the priestly caste both of Egypt and Greece. The Eleusinian mysteries, invented in Egypt and later transferred to Greece, were scenical representations of religion and philosophy which "had previously been painted in hieroglyphic figures to perpetuate them before the discovery of letters. . . . In the first part of this scenery was represented Death, and the destruction of all things. . . . Next the marriage of Cupid and Psyche seems to have shown the reproduction of living nature."[1]

Proteus, he conceives, was a hieroglyphic figure representing Time, "whose form was perpetually changing."[2] Proteus, an Egyptian king or god, is "the principle of all things, and the most ancient of the gods . . . he keeps the keys of Nature . . . all of

[1] Erasmus Darwin, *The Temple of Nature; or, The Origin of Society*, pp. 12-13, note.

[2] *Ibid.*, p. 9, note.

[147]

which might well accord with a figure representing Time."[3]
Further: "Many of the important operations of nature were
shadowed or allegorized in the heathen mythology, as the first
Cupid springing from the Egg of Night, the marriage of Cupid
and Psyche, the Rape of Proserpine, the Congress of Jupiter and
Juno, the Death and Resuscitation of Adonis, etc., many of which
are ingeniously explained in the works of Bacon, Vol. V, p. 47, 4th
Edit., London, 1778. The Egyptians were possessed of many discoveries in philosophy and chemistry before the invention of letters; these were then expressed in hieroglyphic paintings of men
and animals; which after the discovery of the alphabet were described and animated by the poets, and became first the deities of
Egypt, and afterwards of Greece and Rome. Allusions to those
fables were therefore thought proper ornaments to a philosophical
poem, and are occasionally introduced either as represented by the
poets, or preserved on the numerous gems and medallions of
antiquity."[4]

That sea-born Venus symbolizes the origin of life in the sea,
Darwin several times remarks. Venus is the beauty of organic
Nature "which the philosophers of that country [Egypt], the
magi, appear to have discovered to have been elevated by earthquakes from the primeval ocean. But the hieroglyphic figure of
Adonis seems to have signified the spirit of animation or life,
which was perpetually wooed or courted by organic matter, and
which perished and revived alternately. Afterwards the fable
of Adonis seems to have given origin to the first religion promis-
ing a resurrection from the dead."[5] The marriage of Proserpine
and Pluto signifies "the combination or marriage of ethereal spirit
with earthly materials."[6] He then points out the analogy to the
union of oxygen with metallic or inflammable bodies: "From these
fables, which were probably taken from antient hieroglyphics,
there is frequently reason to believe that the Egyptians possessed
much chemical knowledge, which for want of alphabetical writing
perished with their philosophers."[7]

Several times Darwin remarks that "the purer air or ether"
of ancient mythology "was represented by Jupiter, and the inferior air by Juno; and the conjunction of these deities was said
to produce the vernal showers, and procreate all things."[8] In the

[3] Ibid.
[4] Erasmus Darwin, The Botanic Garden, I, xvii-xviii.
[5] Darwin, Temple of Nature, p. 47, note.
[6] Darwin, Botanic Garden, I, 199, note.
[7] Ibid.   [8] Ibid., p. 96, note.

terms of modern meteorology this union of airs is the combination of hydrogen and oxygen to form water: "If we may trust the theory of Mr. Lavoisier concerning the composition and decomposition of water, there would seem another source of thundershowers; and that is, that the two gasses termed oxygene gas or vital air, and hydrogene gas or inflammable air, may exist in the summer atmosphere in a state of mixture but not of combination, and that the electric spark or flash of lightning may combine them and produce water instantaneously."[9]

Further than this the scientific rationalization of myth can scarcely go, though Darwin suggests that Jupiter's unions with Leda, Olympia, and others symbolize the formation of various acids, "pure air, or oxygene uniting with variety of bases."[10] That Shelley could push his own poetic practice in the employment of scientific symbols to such an extreme would offhand be unbelievable. Yet in *Prometheus Unbound* he has done so. The dialogue of the fauns in scene 2 of Act II unmistakably allegorizes the life history of hydrogen in its passage from vegetation to the air, its union with oxygen, and its return as water.[11]

[9] *Ibid.,* p. 63, note.　　　[10] *Ibid.,* p. 96, note.
[11] Grabo, *A Newton Among Poets,* pp. 172-74.

BIBLIOGRAPHY OF WORKS CITED IN TEXT

Beccaria, Giovanni Battista. *A Treatise upon Artificial Electricity.* ... *To Which Is Added, An Essay on the Mild and Slow Electricity Which Prevails in the Atmosphere during Serene Weather. Translated from the Original Italian.* ... London, J. Nourse, 1776.

Bryant, Jacob. *A New System; or, An Analysis of Antient Mythology.* 3rd ed. 6 vols. London, J. Walker, 1807.

Bulstrode, Whitelocke. *An Essay of Transmigration.* ... London, E. H. for Tho. Basset, 1693.

Burnet, John. *Early Greek Philosophy.* London and Edinburgh, Adam and Charles Black, 1892.

Cavallo, Tiberius. *A Complete Treatise on Electricity, in Theory and Practice; with Original Experiments.* 4th ed. 3 vols. London, C. Dilly, 1795.

——— *The Elements of Natural or Experimental Philosophy.* 4 vols. London, T. Cadell and W. Davies, 1803.

——— *A Treatise on Magnetism, in Theory and Practice, with Original Experiments.* 3rd ed., with supp. London, W. & S. Jones, 1800.

Chambers, Ephraim, ed. *Cyclopaedia: or, An Universal Dictionary of Arts and Sciences.* 4 vols. London, W. Strahan, 1778-1786.

Cudworth, Ralph. *The True Intellectual System of the Universe.* A new edition. 4 vols. London, J. F. Dove for Richard Priestley, 1820.

Darwin, Erasmus. *The Botanic Garden.* 4th ed. 2 vols. London, J. Johnson, 1799.

——— *The Temple of Nature; or, The Origin of Society.* London, J. Johnson, 1803.

——— *Zoonomia; or, The Laws of Organic Life.* 2 vols. [Vol. I, 2nd ed., cor.] London, J. Johnson, 1796.

Diodorus Siculus. *The Historical Library of Diodorus the Sicilian.* ... *Trans. by G. Booth.* 2 vols. London, W. M'Dowall for J. Davis, 1814.

Grabo, Carl. *A Newton among Poets: Shelley's Use of Science in Prometheus Unbound.* Chapel Hill, University of North Carolina Press, 1930.

Heraclitus of Ephesus. *The Fragments of the Work of Heraclitus of Ephesus on Nature; trans. by G. T. W. Patrick.* Baltimore, N. Murray, 1889.

Iamblichos. *Theurgia; or, The Egyptian Mysteries . . . trans. . . . by Alexander Wilder.* Greenwich, Conn., The American School of Metaphysics, 1915.

Jennings, Hargrave. *The Rosicrucians, Their Rites and Mysteries.* 3rd ed., newly rev. and cor., and greatly enl. 2 vols. London, J. C. Nimmo, 1887.

King, Edward. *Remarks Concerning Stones.* . . . London, G. Nicol, 1796.

Kunz, George Frederick. *The Magic of Jewels and Charms.* Philadelphia and London, J. B. Lippincott, 1915.

Laplace, Pierre Simon, Marquis de. *The System of the World. Trans. from the French . . . by the Rev. Henry H. Harte.* 2 vols. Dublin, Longman, Rees, Orme, Brown & Green, 1830.

Macrobius, or Philosophy, Science, and Letters in the Year 400. By Thomas Whittaker. Cambridge, The University Press, 1923.

Mesmer, F. A., *Memoires et Aphorismes de.* Supplementary to *Physiologie et Hygiène du Magnétiseur,* par J. J. A. Ricard. Paris, 1844.

Mottelay, Paul Fleury. *Bibliographical History of Electricity and Magnetism.* London, C. Griffin & Company Limited, 1922.

Paracelsus. *The Life of Philippus Theophrastus Bombast of Hohenheim, Known by the Name of Paracelsus, and the Substance of his Teachings . . . by Franz Hartmann.* 2nd ed., rev. and enl. London, K. Paul, Trench, Trubner and Co. Ltd., 1896.

Pavitt, Wm. Thos. and Kate. *The Book of Talismans, Amulets, and Zodiacal Gems.* Philadelphia, D. McKay, 1915.

Pliny. *The Natural History of Pliny. Trans. . . . by . . . John Bostock . . . and H. T. Riley.* 6 vols. London, H. G. Bohn, 1855-57.

Plotinus on the Beautiful . . . trans. by Stephen MacKenna. Stratford-upon-Avon, The Shakespeare Head Press, 1914.

Plutarch's Morals. Theosophical Essays. Trans. by . . . C. W. King. London, G. Bell and Sons, 1889.

Plutarch's Morals. Trans. from the Greek by Several Hands. Cor. and Rev. by Wm. W. Goodwin. 5 vols. Boston, Little, Brown and Company, 1871.

Pococke, Richard, *Travels in Egypt.* [In Pinkerton, John, ed., *A General Collection of the Best and Most Interesting Voyages and Travels.* . . . London, 1808-14, Vol. XV, pp. 163-402.]

Priestley, Joseph. *The History and Present State of Electricity, with Original Experiments.* 4th ed., cor. and enl. London, C. Bathurst, & T. Lowndes, 1775.

Proclus. *The Commentaries of Proclus on the Timaeus of Plato. . . . Trans. from the Greek. By Thomas Taylor.* 2 vols. London, Printed for the Author, 1820.

—— *The Philosophical and Mathematical Commentaries of Proclus, on the First Book of Euclid's Elements. To Which Are Added, A History of the Restoration of Platonic Theology . . . and a Translation from the Greek of Proclus's Theological Elements.* By Thomas Taylor. 2 vols. London, Printed for the Author, 1792.

—— *The Six Books of Proclus, the Platonic Successor, on the Theology of Plato, Trans. from the Greek; to Which a Seventh Book Is Added. . . . By Thomas Taylor.* 2 vols. London, Printed for the Author, 1816.

Rees, Abraham, ed. *The Cyclopaedia; or, Universal Dictionary of Arts, Sciences, and Literature.* 39 vols. London, Longman, Hurst, Rees, Orme, & Brown, 1819-20.

Royal Society of London. *Philosophical Transactions.* London, 1665—.

Savary, Claude Étienne. *Letters on Egypt. . . . Trans. from the French of. . . .* 2nd ed. 2 vols. London, G. G. J. and J. Robinson, 1787.

Snow, Adolph J. *Matter and Gravity in Newton's Physical Philosophy.* London, Oxford University Press, 1926.

Spallanzani, Lazzaro. *Tracts on the Natural History of Animals and Vegetables, Trans. from the Original Italian. By John Graham Dalyell.* 2nd ed. 2 vols. Edinburgh, W. Creech, 1803.

Taylor, Thomas. *The Eleusinian and Bacchic Mysteries. A Dissertation. Ed. . . . by Alexander Wilder.* 4th ed. New York, J. W. Bouton, 1891.

Theophrastus's History of Stones. With an English Version. . . . By John Hill. London, C. Davis, 1746.

Tressan, M. de. *Mythology Compared with History; or, The Fables of the Ancients. . . . Trans. by H. North.* London, T. Cadell and W. Davies, 1797.

INDEX

the Witch, 39; veiled, 43; symbol
of knowledge, 46; preserver of the
infant Horus in myth, 54; consort
of Osiris, 61; name of the moon
goddess, 66; 67; defined by Cudworth, 68; patron of lovers, 70; as
healer, 71; associated with the dews
in Egyptian myth, 73; presiding
deity of moisture, 81; genius of
the Nile, 86; the visible world,
127.

JULIAN, 16.

Juno, 4, 8; the air, 11, 16, 71; one
of manifold names, 15, 48, 55;
fountain of souls, 26, 50; Minerva,
hypostasis of, 46; symbol of the
operations of nature in heathen
myth according to Darwin, 148.

Jupiter, 8; as Dionysus, 15; as the
heaven, 16; position of, 24, 25; as
Apollo, father of Venus, 28; stone
from, 36; as Pan, 42; chemical
symbolism of, 47; association of,
with sapphire, 51; father of Minerva, 72; overthrow of, 79; as
upper air, 148; unions of, with
Leda, etc., 149.

LAPLACE, Pierre Simon, Marquis
de, 33-35.

Latona, 9.

Lavoisier, A. L., 17, 18.

Liquors, medicinal, 44.

Luna, 7.

MACROBIUS, physical rationalization of myth of, 15 *et seq.;* 54.

Magnetism, 53; of ether, 57; as force
of attraction of moon, 76; Gilbert's
theory of, 76; as power of earth
and moon, 77; electric, 78; of
austral lake and magnetic pole, 83;
of crystal vials of Witch, 91 *et
seq.;* Mesmer's theory of, 92; as
force in producing magnetic sleep,
93; a universal principle, 94 *et*

seq.; as influence of planets on hu-
mans, 94; animal, Mesmer's theory
of, 95; difference of animal from
mineral, 96; diagnosis of, in trance,
96; technique of Mesmer with, 97;
confessional dreams under influence of, 101; as the great power
called Mumia, 104; summed in
Witch, 106-07.

Maximus Tyrius, 36.

Medwin, Thomas, 92, 93.

Mesmer, F. A., 92, 93; on the theory
of a universal principle, magnetism,
94 *et seq.;* technique of, 97; 118.

Meteorites, lunar origin of, 34; and
planetoids, 35; as falling stones
sacred to deities, 37.

Metera, 7.

Minerva, 4; name of air, 7; grotto
of, 8; as Isis, 13; goddess of wisdom, 14; as Aphrodite, 16; as
Witch, 24, 44, 48; fountain of
virtues, 26, 50; intellectual nature
of, 38; emerald of, 40; veiled, 43;
knowledge, 46; a virgin, 46; protector of arts, 46; in moon, 66;
triune nature of, 67; mentioned,
68, 71, 72; as air, 72; in Egypt,
87; appearance of, to sick mortals
in dreams, 89; practice of magnetic healing of, 94, 99; nature of,
according to Taylor, 137 *et seq.*

Mithras, 25.

Moon, influence on rising of the Nile,
10, 11, 87; generative power of,
11; source of reason, 12; as Artemis, 13; as goddess, 14; symbol
of Diana, 26; relation of, to lacustrine waters, 27; relation of, to
meteoric stones, 33-34; volcanoes
of, 34; influence of, on atmosphere,
35; seasonal round of, 54; hermaphroditic nature of, 61; physical
attributes of, 63; electric energy of,
64; relation of, to earth, 65; symbol of soul, 66; triune nature of, 66-
67; called ethereal earth by Egyp-